The Thrill of Love

by Amanda Whittington

A NEW VIC PRODUCTION

The Thrill of Love

by Amanda Whittington

The Thrill of Love was first performed on
Friday 22 February 2013 at the New Vic Theatre with the
following cast:

Ruth Ellis	FAYE CASTELOW
Jack Gale	MARK MEADOWS
Sylvia Shaw	HILARY TONES
Vickie Martin	MAYA WASOWICZ
Doris Judd	KATIE WEST

Director	JAMES DACRE
Designer	JONATHAN FENSOM
Associate Director	WILL WRIGHTSON
Lighting Designer	DANIELLA BEATTIE
Sound Designer	JAMES EARLS-DAVIS
Musical Director	MARK MEADOWS
Movement Director	EMILY PIERCY
Dialect Coach	CHARMIAN HOARE
	MARTIN McKELLAN
Casting Associate	ANJI CARROLL CDG
Company Stage Manager	STRUAN SEWELL
Deputy Stage Manager	STEVE HALL
Assistant Stage Manager	HELEN ROLFE

Set and made-props by the New Vic Workshop
Costumes by the New Vic Costume Department

Lighting and sound operated by
Daniella Beattie, James Earls-Davis, Peter Morgan and Matthew Clowes

FOREWORD

As Staffordshire's producing theatre, and Europe's first purpose-built theatre-in-the-round, part of the New Vic's mission is to make great work in this unusual format, often inviting our audiences to explore unconventional ways of making and experiencing theatre. We've flirted with New Circus, with aerial dance, immersive and promenade theatre and installative experiences for preschool children. Physical and visual techniques define our house style, and this year we're exploring outdoor arts.

The other part of our mission is to make a positive difference to our region, one with areas of serious social disadvantage and with severe economic challenges. In the government's Indices of Multiple Deprivation, we regularly find ourselves holding a top-ten position – that's out of 354 local authorities. Children in Stoke-on-Trent have the poorest reading ability in the country.

So, as well as giving our communities artworks to be proud of, there are interventions to be made here, and we have two departments dedicated to making them. Our Education Department work across the curriculum, mainly within the formal education sector. Our *Borderlines* department take the social agenda as their inspiration, working with partners including Newcastle-under-Lyme's Domestic Violence Unit; the Foreign and Commonwealth and Home Office's joint Forced Marriage taskforce; the local constabulary and magistracy.

Working with young people who have become entangled in the criminal-justice system, and seeing them not only applying the tool of theatre to becoming active citizens, but then volunteering to help improve the lives of other individuals and communities, gives the New Vic team a tremendous sense of mission and purpose. We know that we play an important role not only in the cultural but also in the social well-being of our county. At a time when theatre is having to put up a robust defence of its value, these aspects of our work are as important as the significant activity we generate in a sluggish local economy.

So when Amanda Whittington proposed a play about women caught up in the criminal-justice system I knew it was something I wanted us to be involved with. Of course, *The Thrill of Love* has become a much richer play than that, but the provocation at its heart still seems to me to be one about our society's perception of women, and how this affects the justice meted out to them.

Theresa Heskins
Artistic Director

WHO WAS RUTH ELLIS?

Like many 80's teenagers, I discovered Ruth Ellis at the cinema in the film *Dance With a Stranger*. The screenplay was by Shelagh Delaney who'd already captured my imagination with *A Taste of Honey*. Delaney wrote about working-class women in a way that no other playwright had, and her characters were a great influence on my young writing ambitions.

Yet Ruth Ellis is no fictional character. Her story is true and all the more compelling for it.

The bare facts are these: Ruth was executed in 1955, aged twenty-eight, for the murder of her lover, David Blakely. The public outcry and sense of injustice were key factors in the abolition of the death penalty. Ruth Ellis was the last woman to be hanged in Britain and her death was seen as a shocking example of 'the medieval savagery of the law'.

Ruth also made her mark on popular culture. A British 'blonde bombshell', her passionate and tragic affair with an upper-class racing driver was a tabloid reporter's dream. Her lifestyle helped to condemn her in court, as did her lack of remorse. 'It's obvious when I shot him, I intended to kill him,' she told the prosecuting QC. 'No further questions,' he replied. But of course, there are.

Three years ago, Theresa Heskins and I discussed the idea of a Ruth Ellis play for the New Vic. Theatre-in-the-round felt the perfect space to blend the glamorous mythology with sharp social realism. I looked again at films and books on her life but what I saw now was the story they didn't quite tell. Was it jealousy that drove her to kill? I felt sure her obsession with Blakely was a symptom and not the disease. I resolved to forget all I knew, or thought I knew, about the story. Like Inspector Gale, I began with the facts of the case. As I researched, fresh leads were revealed and new dramatic possibilities emerged.

I was drawn to Ruth's best friend, Vickie Martin, a footnote to the accepted story but whose own fate must have had a profound impact on Ruth's state of mind. Her prison psychiatric reports in the National Archives were heartbreaking to read, given what we now know about mental health. Ruth committed a terrible crime but she'd also suffered greatly at the hands of people never brought to justice. In 1955, domestic violence and sexual exploitation had barely been named.

The decision to leave Blakely off-stage gave the narrative in an exciting new form. I created Sylvia Shaw and Doris Judd to explore the all-important emotional truth of Ruth's world. Billie Holiday gave voice to her pain. Then came the language of *film noir,* which is much more than a reference to Ruth's dream of movie stardom. She came to be seen as a *femme fatale*, perhaps in her own mind as well? Gale leads our search for the real woman behind the illusion.

The one sure thing we know is that her brief life still resonates sixty years on. Yet in *The Thrill of Love*, Ruth is not simply a hero, villain or victim. 'They're ordinary girls,' says Sylvia of the hostesses she works with. 'I'd say they're anything but,' replies Gale. This tension lies at the heart of the play. It may be a crime drama, but the mystery remains: do we really know who Ruth Ellis was? Did she? These questions still matter today.

Amanda Whittington

NEW VIC THEATRE

A 600-seater, purpose-built theatre-in-the-round, under Artistic Director, Theresa Heskins, the New Vic offers a varied and adventurous year-round programme of work, including up to nine in-house productions, collaborations and in-tours, and a weekly concert programme of music, dance and comedy. We have wide and deep roots in the community.

We embrace an ethos as inclusive and accessible as our in-the-round auditorium, actively encouraging access to our work, to our building, and to theatre as an art form. We use participatory theatre to support the regeneration of our region by improving life expectations, raising aspiration and achievement, improving the quality of life for disadvantaged people and challenging prejudice.

Our recent productions have included *All Our Daughters?*, launched at Parliament; Alecky Blythe's documentary about aspiration, *Where Have I Been All My Life?*; a rare revival of D.H. Lawrence's *The Widowing of Mrs Holroyd*; and our trademark seasonal show, *A Christmas Carol*.

The company was established in 1962, with its home in a converted Victoria cinema finally became a permanent North Staffordshire home. The New Vic opened in 1986, becoming the first, purpose-built theatre-in-the-round in Europe.

The New Vic is a not-for-profit organisation and a registered charity. We receive financial support from Arts Council England, Newcastle-under-Lyme Borough Council, Staffordshire County Council, and Stoke-on-Trent City Council.

CAST

Faye Castelow (RUTH ELLIS) Theatre includes: *After the Dance, Time and the Conways* (National Theatre); *The Deep Blue Sea, Rattigan's Nijinsky* (Chichester Festival Theatre); *Barefoot in the Park* (national tour); *A Midsummer Night's Dream* (Headlong Theatre); *Cinderella* (Rose, Kingston); *The Importance of Being Earnest* (Hong Kong International Festival); *Leaving, Mountain Hotel* (Orange Tree); *The Guinea Pig Club* (Trafalgar Studios).

Television includes: *Inspector George Gently, Holby City* (BBC).

Film includes: *Revolution*.

Radio includes: *Rumpole of the Bailey, The Merchant of Venice, Missing Dates, Simon Gray* (BBC).

Mark Meadows (JACK GALE & Musical Director) Theatre includes: *The Tempest* (Theatre Royal, Bath); *The Spire, Epsom Downs, The Herbal Bed* (Salisbury Playhouse); *Betty Blue Eyes* (Novello, West End); *The Three Musketeers* (Rose, Kingston); *The Giant* (Hampstead); *A Midsummer Night's Dream, Macbeth* (Open Air Theatre, Regent's Park); *Mary Poppins* (Prince Edward, West End); *Longitude* (Greenwich); *5/11* (Chichester Festival Theatre); *King Lear, Six Pictures of Lee Miller* (Minerva, Chichester); *The Emperor and the Nightingale* (Watermill, Newbury); *High Society* (Sheffield Crucible); *Look Back in Anger, A Streetcar Named Desire, Up the Feeder…, Aeroplane Bones* (Bristol Old Vic).

Television includes: *EastEnders, Doctors, Casualty* (BBC).

Film includes: *Nicholas Nickleby* (United Artists); *High Heels and Lowlifes* (Buena Vista International).

Radio includes: *If Not Now, When?, Torchwood, Lost Souls, Tommy the Voice, Operation Black Buck, The Good Companions, Candide, Company, Pal Joey, My Fair Lady* (BBC Proms); and many more.

Other: Mark is a former Musical Director of the international vocal group The Swingle Singers, for whom he has written many a cappella and orchestral arrangements. He has also written and arranged music and been MD for several theatrical productions.

Mark trained at the Bristol Old Vic Theatre School.

Hilary Tones (SYLVIA SHAW) Theatre includes: *Swallows and Amazons* (West End and UK tour); *A Small Family Business* (Clwyd Theatr, Cymru); *Original Sin* (Haymarket, Basingstoke); *The Lady in the Van* (Salisbury Playhouse); *Romeo and Juliet* (Middle Temple Hall); *Pericles, Measure for Measure, Macbeth* (Shakespeare's Globe); *Mary Stuart, Shirley Valentine* (Derby Playhouse); *Absolutely (Perhaps!)* (Wyndham's, West End); *The Magistrate, She's in Your Hands* (Royal Exchange, Manchester); *Twelfth Night* (Oxford Stage Company); *The Visit* (Chichester Festival Theatre); *The Fire Raisers, Liberation of Skopje* (Riverside Studios); *Rosencrantz and Guildernstern are Dead* (Dramski Theatre, Skopje, Macedonia), *The Three Musketeers* (Sheffield Crucible); *An Ideal Husband* (Lyric, Belfast); *Private View* (Rokoko, Prague); *Salt of the Earth, Woyzeck, Can't Stand Up for Falling Down* (Hull Truck); *Hamlet, Romeo and Juliet, Have* (RSC).

Television includes: *Wire in the Blood, Criminal Justice, Casualty, The Bill, Holby City, Doctors, Judge John Deed, Tenth Kingdom, Body Story, Silent Witness, Persuasion, Coronation Street, Gaudy Night.*

Film includes: *Volume, The Great Expectation of Robert Carmichael.*

Hilary trained at Central School of Speech and Drama.

Maya Wasowicz (VICKIE MARTIN) Theatre includes: *The Faith Machine* (Royal Court); *Design for Living* (Old Vic); *Death of a Salesman* (West Yorkshire Playhouse); *Twelfth Night* (RSC).

Television includes: *Wallander, Waking the Dead, Mutual Friends* (BBC).

Film includes: *Huge.*

Maya trained at Guildhall School of Music and Drama.

Katie West (DORIS JUDD) Theatre credits include: *A Taste of Honey* (Sheffield Crucible); *Glory Dazed* (Underbelly, Edinburgh Festival); *Once Upon a Time in Wigan, 65 Miles* (Hull Truck); *Punk Rock* (Royal Exchange, Manchester/Lyric Hammersmith/tour); *Blithe Spirit* (Royal Exchange, Manchester); *Auricular* (Theatre503); *Sense* (Company of Angels); *For One Night Only/In One Minute* (BBC Manchester/Contact, Manchester); *Manchester* (Contact, Manchester). Theatre workshops include: *Britannia Rules The Waves, I Started A Fire* (Royal Exchange, Manchester); *We Say Au Revoir* (Lyric Hammersmith).

Film and television includes: *You* (ITV); *United* (World Productions); *Doctors* (BBC); *Angie* (Creative Lab).

Katie trained at Drama Centre London.

CREATIVE TEAM

Amanda Whittington (Writer) is a popular dramatist whose plays include *Be My Baby*, originally produced by Soho Theatre and subsequently staged throughout the UK. *Ladies' Day* and its sequel *Ladies Down Under* (Hull Truck/UK tours) are also widely performed. Forthcoming new work includes *The Dug Out* for Splice Theatre, which opens at the Tobacco Factory Bristol in May. *My Judy Garland Life* (adapted from the book by Susie Boyt) will be staged at Nottingham Playhouse in early 2014. *Ladies' Day* will also be produced by Oldham Coliseum in May this year. Past stage productions includes *Satin 'n' Steel* (Nottingham Playhouse/Bolton Octagon); *Bollywood Jane* (Leicester Haymarket/West Yorkshire Playhouse); *Tipping the Velvet* (adapted from the novel by Sarah Waters/Guildhall School of Music and Drama); *Saturday Night and Sunday Morning* (New Perspectives); and *The Wills' Girls* (Tobacco Factory, Bristol). Amanda writes regularly for Radio 4 and her recent radio dramas include Woman's Hour series *Once Upon a Time* and *Paradise Place*, *Louisa's* (Weird Tales) and *The Nine Days Queen* (Afternoon Drama). She began her writing career as a journalist for titles including *New Statesman and Society* and *The Face*. She has also written for television and was joint winner of the BBC2 Dennis Potter Award in 2001. Her plays are published by Nick Hern Books.

James Dacre (Director) was previously Artistic Associate at the New Vic Theatre where his directing credits include *Desire Under the Elms*, *Copenhagen* and *Bus Stop*, which transferred to the Stephen Joseph Theatre. Recent directing credits include *The Accrington Pals* (Royal Exchange, Manchester); *King James Bible* (National Theatre); *Orpheus and Eurydice* (National Youth Theatre/Old Vic); *The Unconquered* (Stellar Quines, UK tour/Off-Broadway transfer) and *Nightshifts* (Traverse). James's world-premiere production of *The Mountaintop* (Theatre503/Trafalgar Studios) won the 2010 Olivier Award for Best New Play and was nominated for a further five awards; *Precious Little Talent* (Trafalgar Studios) won Best Play at the 2011 London Theatre Festival Awards and was nominated for an Evening Standard Award; *Judgement Day* (The Print Room) won an Ian Charleson Best Actress commendation and *As You Like It* (Shakespeare's Globe, European tour and 2012 revival) shared the UK Theatre Awards' 2011 Renee Stepham Award for touring. Work Off-Broadway includes *Baal*, *The Error of Their Ways*, *Work* and *Come and Go*. James has directed new plays by Mike Poulton, Roy Williams, Katori Hall, Dic Edwards, Suzan Lori Parks, Ed Kemp, Molly Davies, Torben Betts, Bekah Brunstetter and Ella Hickson amongst others. He is an Associate Director at Theatre503, has been awarded Fulbright and Schubert Fellowships in Theatre Directing and trained on the ITV/Channel 4 Regional Theatre Director's Scheme. He is currently preparing *Julius Caesar* (National Theatre Studio) with Hydrocracker and Blast Theory and the European premiere of Amy Herzog's *4000 Miles* (Bath Theatre Royal).

Jonathan Fensom (Designer) Jonathan's theatre productions include: *The Accrington Pals* (Royal Exchange, Manchester); *Henry V, Hamlet, Henry IV Part 1 & 2, King Lear, Love's Labour's Lost* (Shakespeare's Globe); *Canvas* (Chichester Festival Theatre); *As You Like It* (Rose, Kingston); *Goat* (Traverse); *Six Degrees of Separation, National Anthems* (Old Vic); *Brighton Beach Memoirs* (Watford); *Philadelphia Here I Come* (Gaiety Theatre, Dublin); *A Midsummer Night's Dream* (Canada); *Our Boys, Rain Man, Some Girls, Twelfth Night, Smaller, What the Butler Saw, Abigail's Party, East* (West End); *Swan Lake* (San Francisco Ballet); *Journey's End* (West End/Broadway); *The American Plan, Pygmalion* (Broadway); *Becky Shaw, The Homecoming, Big White Fog* (Almeida); *Happy Now?, The Mentalists, Burn/Citizenship/Chatroom* (National Theatre); *In the Club, Born Bad, Abigail's Party, In Arabia We'd All Be Kings, What the Butler Saw* (Hampstead); *Duck, Talking to Terrorists, The Sugar Syndrome* (Royal Court); *Kindertransport, Breakfast with Emma* (Shared Experience); *The Tempest* (Tron); *Crown Matrimonial* (Guildford/tour); *The Faith Healer* (Gate, Dublin/Broadway); *God of Hell* (Donmar Warehouse); *M.A.D., Little Baby Nothing* (Bush); *Be My Baby* (Soho); *Small Family Business, Little Shop of Horrors* (West Yorkshire Playhouse); *My Night With Reg, Dealer's Choice* (Birmingham Rep); *Candide, After the Dance, Hay Fever* (Oxford Stage Company). Jonathan was the Associate Scenic Designer on Disney's *The Lion King*, which premiered at the New Amsterdam Theatre on Broadway in November 1997 and has subsequently opened worldwide. His set design for *Journey's End* was nominated for a Tony Award in 2007. Upcoming work includes *The American Plan* (Bath Theatre Royal); *A Midsummer Night's Dream, King Lear, Gabriel* (Shakespeare's Globe); *Pygmalion* (national tour).

Will Wrightson (Associate Director) Recent theatre includes, as Director: *Don't Exaggerate* (Jermyn Street Theatre, London); *Mudlarks* (HighTide Festival/Theatre503/Bush); *Up With (Some) People* (Soho); *The Five O'Clock Club* (Theatre503); *Little Malcolm and His Struggle Against the Eunuchs* (Edinburgh Fringe). As Associate Director and Producer: *Lingua Franca* (Finborough, London/59E59 Theaters, New York); *Threshold* (Edinburgh Fringe). As Assistant Director: *The Caretaker* (Adelaide Festival, San Francisco and BAM, New York); *Judgement Day* (The Print Room); *Hot Mess* (Latitude Festival/Arcola Tent); *Precious Little Talent* (Trafalgar Studios). Will is an Associate Artist at HighTide Festival Theatre and a National Theatre Connections Director.

Daniella Beattie (Lighting Designer) For the New Vic Theatre as Resident Lighting Designer: *A Christmas Carol, A Bright Fine Day Today, Far From the Madding Crowd, Alfie, Alice in Wonderland, And a Nightingale Sang, The Glass Menagerie* (with Oldham Coliseum), *The Admirable Crichton, Peter Pan, Desire Under the Elms, Bleak House, Copenhagen, Alphabetical Order, The Lion, the Witch and the Wardrobe, Bouncers, The Wicked Lady* (Best Lighting Design, TMA Awards 2009), *A Taste of Honey, Honeymoon Suite, A Voyage Round My Father, Arabian Nights, Dangerous Corner, Flamingoland, Great Expectations, Laurel and Hardy, Les Liaisons Dangereuses, On Golden Pond, Jamaica Inn, Oliver!, The Prime of Miss Jean Brodie, Stags and Hens, The Safari Party, One Flew Over the Cuckoo's Nest, Smoke, A Christmas Carol, Sizwe Banzi is Dead, As You Like It, East Lynne, The Graduate, Kitty and Kate, Pinocchio, To Kill a Mocking Bird, Once We Were Mothers, Can't Pay? Won't Pay!, Amadeus, Beauty and the Beast, Kes, Carmen, Once a Catholic, The Lonesome West, Love Me Slender, The Duchess of Malfi, The Marriage of Figaro, Outside Edge, The Beauty Queen of Leenane, Pump Boys and Dinettes, Romeo and Juliet, Billy Liar, All That Trouble That We Had, Cleo, Camping, Emmanuelle and Dick, Ham, Big Maggie, Who's Afraid of Virginia Woolf?* Other theatre includes: *Romeo and Juliet, The Tempest* (Northern Broadsides); *The Mikado* (Orange Tree, Richmond). Daniella trained at Bretton Hall (University of Leeds).

James Earls-Davis (Sound Designer) For the New Vic: all main-house sound designs since 1987 including: *Talking Heads, A Christmas Carol, A Fine Bright Day Today, Far From the Madding Crowd, Where Have I Been All My Life?, Alice in Wonderland, The Glass Menagerie, The Admirable Crichton, Spring and Port Wine, The Rivals, Bus Stop, Peter Pan, Bleak House, Alphabetical Order, Humble Boy, And a Nightingale Sang, The Lion, the Witch and the Wardrobe, Bouncers, The Daughter-in-Law, Dumb Show, A Taste of Honey, Honeymoon Suite, The Price, A Voyage Round My Father, Arabian Nights, The Weir, Dangerous Corner, Flamingoland, Don Giovanni, Great Expectations, Laurel and Hardy, Be My Baby, Cider With Rosie, Les Liaisons Dangereuses, Jamaica Inn, The Glee Club, Oliver!, One Flew Over the Cuckoo's Nest, Abigail's Party, A Christmas Carol, Sizwe Banzi Is Dead, As You Like It, Four Nights in Knaresborough* and *Carmen.* Original music includes: *A Fine Bright Day Today, Proof, Desire Under the Elms, Copenhagen, Blue/Orange, Misery, Dealer's Choice, Romeo and Juliet, Broken Glass* (solo); *Talking Heads, Smoke, Once We Were Mothers, Kes, All That Trouble That We Had* (with Russell Gregory); *The Wicked Lady, Romeo and Juliet, A Fine Bright Day Today* (with Sue Moffat). Other sound design and/or original music includes: *The Game* (Northern Broadsides); *A Number* (Library Theatre, Manchester); *These Four Streets* (Birmingham Rep); *Rebecca, Frozen* (Theatre by the Lake, Keswick); *King Macbeth, Silent Anger, Homefront, Sticks and Stones* (Reveal Theatre Co); *Twelfth Night* (Belgrade, Coventry); *Her Big Chance* (Harrogate); several sound designs and/or original music for New Vic *Borderlines* and Education, and soundtracks for community arts projects and films.

Emily Piercy (Movement Director) Theatre credits include, as Assistant Choreographer: *Privates on Parade* (Noel Coward, West End); *Carmen* (Royal Danish Opera); *Salome* (Royal Opera House). As Revival Choreographer: *Carmen* (Royal Danish Opera and Opera Vest, Norway). As actor: *La bohème, Agrippina* (ENO); *Ruby and The Big Top* (Bea Theatre); *Johnno* (Derby Playhouse); *Red Red Shoes* (Unicorn Children's Theatre); *Aida* (Earl's Court). As dancer: *Dancer and the Magic Piano* (Arthur Pita Company). As Director *Ruby and The Big Top* (Bea Theatre). For New Adventures: *Play Without Words* (National Theatre); *Nutcracker!* (Sadlers Wells Theatre); *Car Man* (Old Vic); *Cinderella* (Piccadilly/Los Angeles); *Swan Lake* (Piccadilly/Los Angeles, Broadway). Film and television credits include: *Swan Lake* (BBC/NVC Film); *Mrs Hartley and the Growth Centre* (BBC Screen 2); *Red Riding Hood* (BBC); *The Magic Flute* (dir. Kenneth Branagh).

Anji Carroll CDG (Casting Associate) For the New Vic: *A Christmas Carol, The Widowing of Mrs Holroyd, A Bright Fine Day Today, Where Have I Been All My Life?, Alice in Wonderland, The Glass Menagerie, The Admirable Crichton, Spring and Port Wine, Proof, The Rivals, Bus Stop, Peter Pan, Desire Under the Elms, Copenhagen, Bleak House, Dumb Show, Honeymoon Suite.* Theatre includes: *Judgement Day* (The Print Room); *Precious Little Talent* (Best Play at the London Theatre Festival Awards 2011; Trafalgar Studios); *Othello, Richard III* (Ludlow Festival); *The Ladykillers, Twelfth Night, The Deep Blue Sea, Macbeth, The Notebook of Trigorin* (Northcott Theatre); *The Wizard of Oz, Who's Afraid of Virginia Woolf?, Antigone, The Beggar's Opera, A Chorus of Disapproval, Henry IV Part 1 & 2, The Wind in the Willows, Betrayal* (Bristol Old Vic). Television credits include: *Inside the Titanic* (Channel 5); *The Cup* (BBC2); *The Bill* (over 50 episodes); *The Sarah Jane Adventures – Invasion of the Bane*; two series of *London's Burning* (32 episodes) and *The Knock* (4 x 90-minute episodes). Other credits include: feature films *Papadopoulos & Sons, West Is West, Mrs Ratcliffe's Revolution, Out of Depth, The Jolly Boys' Last Stand.* Drama documentary includes: *Curiosity: What Sank Titanic?, Mayday, Joan of Arc.* BBC Radio 4 political drama series *Number 10.* Anji is a member of the Casting Directors' Guild of Great Britain.

NEW VIC STAFF

Artistic Director Theresa Heskins
Executive Director Fiona Wallace

Financial Controller Sarah Townshend
Finance Manager Irene Goodwin
Accounts Assistant Tina Pardoe
Administration Manager
Tracey Wainwright
Fundraising Officer Victoria Martin
Administration Officer Martin Hayward
Administrative Assistant
Charlotte Moulder
Creative People & Places
Interim Producer Gemma Thomas

Production Manager Steve O'Brien
Company Stage Manager Struan Sewell
Deputy Stage Managers
Steve Hall, Vicky Laker
Assistant Stage Managers
Helen Rolfe, Natalie Haínon
Student on Attachment
Tim Henshaw
Head of Technical Dept/
Sound Designer James Earls-Davis
Chief Electrician & Resident
Lighting Designer Daniella Beattie
Deputy Chief Electrician Peter Morgan
Sound & Lighting Technician
Matthew Clowes

Head of Design Lis Evans
Head of Workshop Laura Clarkson
Propmaker & Scenic Artist
Denise Sewell
Production Carpenters
Louise Rider, Lee Wood

Costume Supervisor Pat Blenkarn
Deputy Costume Supervisor/Cutter
Alison Sunnuck
Deputy Costume Supervisor/
Cutter (Maternity Leave cover)
Sarah Thorne
Costume Cutter
Karen Norcross-Downs
Costume Assistant Deborah Hall
Senior Costume Technician /Hairdresser
Eileen Spong
Costume Technician/Maker
Christina Whitehill

Head of Marketing & Business
Development John Morton
Marketing Manager & Graphic Designer
Candida Kelsall
Press Officer & Online Editor
Claire Walker
Marketing Officer Kay Wilson
Web & Graphic Designer Kevin Hegarty
Box Office & IT Manager Pete Leverett
Deputy Box Office Manager
Mandy Fletcher
Sales Officers Emma Christopher,
Jennifer Dunn, Lyndsay Rushton

***Borderlines* Director** Susan Moffat
Outreach Stage & Technical Manager
Rachel Reddihough
Young People's Theatre Company
Director & Theatre Practitioner
Filiz Ozcan
Theatre Practitioner
Julianna Skarżyńska
***Borderlines* Administrative Assistant**
Adhia Mahmood
Administrative Assistant
(Maternity Leave cover) Alison Tinning

Head of Education Jill Rezzano
Education Administration
& Project Manager Lynn Parry
Education Theatre Practitioner
Sarah Richardson
Youth Theatre Director
& Education Practitioner Katherine Hughes
Chaperones Mary Keogh, Roma Read

Front of House Manager David Sunnuck
Deputy Front of House Manager
Johanna Thomson
Duty Managers Mandy Fletcher,
Sarah Oksiuk, Debbie Slater
Theatre Attendants
Mandy Clarke, Maureen Cuell, Barbara
Hargreaves, Angela James, Pauline Johnson,
David Kirk, Peter Palmer, Dorothy Roche,
Roy Smith, Gwynneth Stirland, Nicola Stones,
David Symes
Senior Theatre Premises
& Fire Warden Paula Middleton
Theatre Premises & Fire Warden
Pauline Cregg, Philip Stanworth, David Symes
Senior Cleaner Margaret Hulstone
Cleaners Elaine Caldwell, Maureen Kimberly,
Craig McLaughlin, Barbara Wickes
Car Park Attendants Russell Gregory,
Dan James, Antony Lane, Alex Matthews,
Ricardio Sentulio

Catering Manager Pauline Bentley
Chef Paul Dickens
Senior Catering Assistant Paula Prince
Catering Assistants Jessica Beardmore,
Michaela Everill, Bethan Hanley, Clair
Hammersley, Calum Hassall, Tom James, Pam
Jones, Carol McDonald, Patricia Oliver, Doreen
Punshon, Jemma Stubbs, Pat Whimpanny
Bar Supervisor Rob Punshon
Bar Staff Rebecca Charlesworth, Sandy Davies,
Lorna Denny, Sue English, James Gregory, Kathy
Jackson, Alex Matthews, Fran Pardoe, Maureen
Rooney, Ashley Trevor

Maintenance Technician Mike Unwin
Gardener Ron Gray
Maintenance Assistant Rory Evans

THE THRILL OF LOVE

Amanda Whittington

Characters

RUTH ELLIS, *a nightclub hostess*

JACK GALE, *a detective inspector*

SYLVIA SHAW, *a nightclub manageress*

VICKIE MARTIN, *a model and actress*

DORIS JUDD, *a charwoman*

Staging should be fluid and filmic, with the changing locations imaginatively revealed.

The recordings suggested in the play are by Billie Holiday, subject to the rights being available.

The Thrill of Love *is based on a true story. Some scenes, characters and events have been included or altered for dramatic purposes.*

This text went to press before the end of rehearsals and so may differ slightly from the play as performed.

ACT ONE

Scene One

From the scratch and hiss of a gramophone comes Billie Holiday singing 'T'ain't Nobody's Business If I Do'.

RUTH ELLIS *appears in a hazy bedroom light. She wears her undergarments and spike heels. She puts on a skirt and blouse.*

As she dresses, the record begins to jump. RUTH *doesn't allow it to distract her.*

RUTH *puts on her coat, ties on a headscarf and puts her handbag over her arm.*

RUTH *looks in the mirror, her gaze unflinching. We see the archetypal blonde bombshell, the femme fatale.*

RUTH *puts on her spectacles, reaches into her handbag and pulls out a gun. She feels the unfamiliar weight of it in her hand.*

A figure (JACK GALE) *emerges behind her.*

The record hits a scratch and begins to repeat the same phrase. RUTH *takes the gun in both hands and extends her arms, holding it before her.*

RUTH. David?

RUTH *turns to the figure and fires the gun.*

Six gunshots sound in an irregular pattern. They bring a cacophony of cries in the street, police bells and flashing blue lights.

Scene Two

GALE *takes off his overcoat and trilby hat. As the chaos subsides, he addresses the audience. He is military-sharp, with a hint of the streets.*

GALE. Hampstead Station, 5th Division, eleventh of April, 1955. I'm at home with my girls: Ella, Billie, Sarah Vaughan. Whisky and lemon, bit of a cold coming on. Curtains closed, rain on the window, telephone rings at a quarter-to-ten. 'You need to get down here, sir. Now.'

RUTH *sits in a chair in the centre of the floor.*

Midnight, Easter Sunday. But if Christ really rose from the dead, He's not in the city tonight.

GALE *turns his attention to* RUTH.

Mrs Ellis? I've just seen the dead body of David Blakely at Hampstead Mortuary. I understand you know something about it?

RUTH *doesn't respond.*

Mrs Ellis, I've just –

RUTH. I am guilty. I'm rather confused.

GALE *looks to the audience.*

GALE. She's given a statement. Clear voice, cool as ice. But it's my job to turn up the heat.

GALE *opens the file and reads from the statement.*

'I understand what's been said. I am guilty. I'm rather confused.'

RUTH. Yes.

GALE. 'About two years ago, I met David Blakely when I was manageress of The Little Club, Knightsbridge. My flat was above that. I had known him for about a fortnight when I started to live with him and – '

RUTH. That's not quite... He lived with me.

GALE *amends the statement and continues to read, monitoring* RUTH*'s responses as he does.*

GALE. 'He lived with me... and has done so until last year, when he went away to Le Mans for about three weeks, motor racing. He came back to me and remained living with me until Good Friday morning. He left about ten o'clock a.m. and promised to be back by eight p.m. to take me out. I waited until half-past nine and he had not phoned, although he always had done in the past.'

RUTH. Yes.

GALE. 'I was rather worried, as he'd had trouble with his racing car and had been drinking. I rang some friends of his named Findlater at Hampstead but they told me he was not there.'

RUTH *sneezes.*

RUTH. Excuse me.

GALE *hands* RUTH *a white handkerchief from his pocket.*

GALE. It's clean.

RUTH. I'm sure.

GALE. 'I took a taxi to Hampstead, where I saw David's car outside Findlater's flat on 28 Tanza Road. I telephoned from nearby, and when my voice was recognised they hung up on me. I went to the flat and continually rang the doorbell. I became very furious and went to David's car and pushed in three of the side windows.'

RUTH. Correct.

GALE. 'David did not come home on Saturday, and at nine o'clock this morning – Sunday – I phoned again, and Mr Findlater answered. I said to him – '

RUTH. 'I hope you are having an enjoyable holiday.'

GALE. 'And was about to say – '

RUTH. 'Because you have ruined mine.'

GALE. 'And he banged the receiver down.'

RUTH. Hard.

GALE. Shall I add…?

RUTH. No.

GALE. 'I waited all day today for David to phone but he did not do so. About eight o'clock this evening, I put my son Andréa to bed.'

RUTH. Yes.

GALE. 'I then took a gun which was given to me about three years ago in a club by a man whose name I do not remember.'

RUTH. No.

RUTH *picks at the stitching of the handkerchief.*

GALE. The club or the man, Mrs Ellis?

RUTH. J.

GALE. J?

RUTH. Your initial.

RUTH *nods to an embroidered letter.*

GALE. John. But I'm known here as Jack.

RUTH. Jack…

GALE. Gale. Detective Inspector.

RUTH. Jack Gale.

GALE. You say the gun was security for money but you accepted it as a curiosity?

RUTH. Yes.

GALE. You didn't know it was loaded when it was given to you but you knew the next morning when you looked at it.

RUTH. Yes.

GALE *glances at the statement.*

GALE. 'When I put the gun in my bag, I intended to find David and shoot him.'

RUTH. Yes.

GALE. You know what that comment implies?

RUTH. It doesn't imply anything, sir. It's a statement of fact.

RUTH *begins to fold the handkerchief as if it's a napkin.*

GALE. 'I took a taxi to Tanza Road, and as I arrived, David's car drove away. I dismissed the taxi and walked back down the road to the nearest pub, where I saw David's car. I waited outside until he came out. David went to his door to open it. I was a little way away from him. He turned and saw me and then turned away from me. And I took the gun from my bag and I shot him.'

RUTH *quietly admires the folded handkerchief.*

RUTH. Yes.

GALE. And then?

RUTH. I've explained.

GALE. Not to me.

RUTH *looks up.*

RUTH. David turned and ran around the car. I thought I'd missed him, so I fired again. He was still running and I fired a third time. I don't remember firing any more but I must have done.

GALE. There were six shots. One ricocheted off the footway.

RUTH. Oh, really?

GALE. Hit a passer-by in the hand.

RUTH. I remember…

GALE. Go on.

RUTH. He was lying face down. Bleeding badly. It seemed ages before an ambulance came…

GALE. Mrs Ellis?

RUTH. A man came up. I said: 'Will you call the police and an ambulance?' He said: 'I am a policeman.' I said: 'Please take this gun and arrest me.'

GALE. Do you wish to say anything more?

RUTH. No, sir.

GALE. Are you sure, Mrs Ellis?

RUTH. Quite sure.

> GALE *takes a long look at* RUTH, *who holds his gaze.*

GALE. 'This statement has been read over to me, and it is true.'

> RUTH *takes off her spectacles.*

RUTH. Yes.

> *The cold white flashbulb of a police camera explodes at* RUTH: *two into her face, two each side, in the pattern of the gunshots.*

Scene Three

GALE *crosses into the warm glow of The Court Club.*

GALE. The truth: rarely pure, never simple. Well, not on her side of town. She might see it winking in gas lamps or scurrying under the tracks. She may catch its eye in a shopfront then turn up her collar, walk on. Cos this is a girl 'on the up'. No more the Depression and one ragged dress, no more the Luftwaffe's reign. Tonight, she's in W1, sir. Spike heels heading down to The Court Club, Duke Street.

> SYLVIA SHAW, *a doyenne of the London club scene, crosses the floor with a bag of loose change.* GALE *turns his attention to her.*

She came here in…?

SYLVIA. Don't know, exactly.

GALE. Two, three, four years ago?

SYLVIA. Maybe more.

GALE. And she left for The Little?

SYLVIA. Few months back.

GALE. Workmates?

SYLVIA. She had 'em, yes.

GALE. Names?

  SYLVIA *empties the change onto a table to count*.

SYLVIA. Peggy, Margaret, Vickie, Dora, Anne –

GALE. Surnames.

SYLVIA. You forget.

GALE. You're the manageress.

SYLVIA. Girls come and go. Ten-a-penny.

GALE. Cash-in-hand, is it? Back-pocket stuff?

SYLVIA. What are you asking, Inspector?

GALE. Just what you're running, that's all.

SYLVIA. This is a gentleman's club.

GALE. And nothing deceives like an obvious fact. You of all
    people know that.

SYLVIA. Do I?

GALE. When did you meet her, Miss Shaw?

SYLVIA. '48? '50, perhaps?

GALE. Before she married?

SYLVIA. Of course.

GALE. To one of your members, I'm told.

SYLVIA. Occupational hazard.

GALE. A dentist.

SYLVIA. Allegedly.

GALE. Oh?

SYLVIA. Let's just say you'd rather have toothache.

GALE *picks up the eponymously named LP, 'Billie Holiday', and reads the sleeve.*

GALE. Lady Day.

SYLVIA. Nothing gets past you, does it?

GALE. She does. She gets right under my skin.

GALE *meets her eye.*

SYLVIA. I know what you're doing, Inspector.

GALE. Oh?

SYLVIA. Oh, yes. I've played this game longer than you.

GALE. What game?

SYLVIA. You started out on the beat, am I right? Nicking tarts on Old Compton Street, walking the West End like them.

GALE. Years back.

SYLVIA. But some of them girls are still out there, aren't they? Still twirling the same set of keys.

GALE. Of course.

SYLVIA. 'Inspector now, eh? Clever boy. Coming up for a cuppa?'

GALE. They're contacts.

SYLVIA. Close contacts and why not? Don't hurt every once in a while.

GALE. You're sailing close to the wind, Miss Shaw.

SYLVIA. Aren't we all, dear?

Beat.

GALE. George Ellis –

SYLVIA. I've nothing to say about him.

GALE. Would you rather do this at the station?

SYLVIA. Arresting me, are you? For what?

GALE. Sit down.

SYLVIA. Slander and libel?

GALE. Sit!

> GALE *slams a chair in the middle of the floor.* SYLVIA *archly complies.*
>
> David Blakely.

SYLVIA. What about him?

GALE. You tell me?

SYLVIA. Tall, dark and handsome.

GALE. Not on the slab.

SYLVIA. Well, that's love for you, that's why you warn 'em against it.

GALE. You do?

SYLVIA. Not that they listen, of course.

GALE. She says they met at The Little?

SYLVIA. She would.

GALE. Did you know him? Did he ever come here?

SYLVIA. He was here, there and everywhere. That was the trouble for her.

GALE. Green-eyed monster, then? She couldn't have him so nobody could?

SYLVIA. I daresay but she made her own bed.

GALE. We're not so sure about that.

SYLVIA. Oh, come on, it's a cut-and-dried case.

> GALE *flips open his pocketbook.*

GALE. 'I took a gun which was given to me about three years ago in a club by a man whose name I do not remember.'

SYLVIA. She said that?

GALE. Sworn statement.

SYLVIA. Which club?

GALE. That's what I'm here to find out.

SYLVIA. Not mine.

GALE. No?

SYLVIA. Not mine.

   SYLVIA *returns to her table.*

GALE. How do you know?

SYLVIA. London's littered with guns from the war.

GALE. See a lot of them, do you?

SYLVIA. Not here.

GALE. Shall we look at your membership list?

SYLVIA. I'm afraid that's not possible.

GALE. Why?

SYLVIA. This is a private establishment.

GALE. This is a capital crime.

   Beat.

SYLVIA. I read in the *News of the World* she's confessed.

GALE. She sang like a canary. But I hear the static as well as the song.

SYLVIA. Static?

GALE. What man? Which club?

   Beat.

SYLVIA. She's taking the rap for a bloke?

GALE. She is if she doesn't start talking.

SYLVIA. I couldn't shut the girl up.

GALE. And what did she tell you?

Beat.

SYLVIA. I don't speak to the police.

GALE. On the record, at least?

SYLVIA *nods.* GALE *closes his pocketbook.*

SYLVIA. See? You do know the game.

GALE. Whisky and soda, Miss Shaw.

SYLVIA *fixes a drink as* GALE *puts the needle onto a gramphone record.*

Scene Four

The scratchy opening bars of 'Love for Sale' by Billie Holiday plays. SYLVIA *and the* COMPANY *sprinkle debris across the floor, upturn chairs and scatter bottles.*

GALE. The halcyon days of The Court. Smog falls like a shroud and like many before her, a young girl comes in from the cold.

VICKIE MARTIN *steals in, a handkerchief to her mouth and a suitcase in her hand.* GALE *watches and listens.*

VICKIE. Excuse me?

SYLVIA. We're shut.

VICKIE. Miss Shaw, is it?

SYLVIA. Come back at three.

VICKIE. But it's took us an hour from the Tube.

As SYLVIA *turns, a hail of Camera Club flashbulbs illuminate* VICKIE's *gamine smile.*

SYLVIA. Where've you come from?

VICKIE. Bloody Bond Street, that's all. Smog gets worse every year.

SYLVIA. Who sent you, I mean?

VICKIE. Mr Conley. He says he owns the place, says you've got work.

SYLVIA. Does he now?

VICKIE. Have you?

SYLVIA. We're in need of a char.

VICKIE. Not that kind of work.

Beat.

SYLVIA. Ambitious girl, are you?

VICKIE. You have to be, don't you? In this life.

SYLVIA. You do. Try the dress shop next door.

VICKIE. But he says you've got rooms here, an' all.

SYLVIA *sweeps broken glass from the floor.*

SYLVIA. Known him long, have you? Morrie?

VICKIE. I met him last night.

SYLVIA. Camera Club.

VICKIE. How can you tell?

SYLVIA. Sixth sense.

VICKIE. I had to leave where I was, see?

SYLVIA. Out the back?

VICKIE. Weren't my fault, the landlord's a crook. I've been sleeping on floors for a month.

SYLVIA. Why don't you go home, then?

VICKIE. I will do, one day. In a silver Rolls Royce, just you wait.

SYLVIA. So where is it, exactly? Your home.

VICKIE. Egham, Surrey.

SYLVIA. What's your name?

VICKIE. Valerie.

SYLVIA. Valerie…?

VICKIE. Mewes.

SYLVIA. Got a ring on your finger?

VICKIE. No fear.

SYLVIA. What, no fella at all?

VICKIE. I'm a free spirit, aren't I?

SYLVIA. I see. But you know how to mix with the men?

VICKIE. Oh, I'll talk to anyone, me. And I've won trophies for dance. Latin, ballroom, the lot. Cha-cha-cha.

   VICKIE *demonstrates a dance step.*

SYLVIA. Mental arithmetic?

VICKIE. Top of the class.

SYLVIA. Three G and Ts, fifteen shillings and a bottle of champagne, three pounds. Snowballs all round for the girls, thirty bob. What's on the tab?

VICKIE. Five pounds and five bob.

SYLVIA. Date of birth?

VICKIE. Second of August 1931.

SYLVIA. So that makes you –

VICKIE. Leo the lion, and you?

   Beat.

SYLVIA. Scorpio.

VICKIE. Deep. Passionate. Impulsive.

SYLVIA. Leave a number, dear. I'll let you know.

VICKIE. I don't have a number.

SYLVIA. All right, come back next week.

VICKIE. But, Miss Shaw, I've nowhere to stay.

SYLVIA. I can't help you with that.

VICKIE. Mr Conley assured me you could.

SYLVIA. Oh?

VICKIE. He said I've a heart-stopping smile.

SYLVIA. Course he did. There's a room on the top floor.

VICKIE. You won't regret it, Miss Shaw!

SYLVIA. Five pounds a week with a couple of dresses to start.

VICKIE. Five pounds?

SYLVIA. We open at three. You'll sit with the members, find out what interests them: sport, history, current affairs.

VICKIE. Current affairs?

SYLVIA. You're mixing with well-to-do gents here. Public school, officer-class.

VICKIE. Am I?

SYLVIA. So you study the newspapers, all right? You laugh at their jokes and listen intent to their stories.

VICKIE. And tell 'em a few of my own.

SYLVIA. Make sure their glasses are full. Encourage a supper for two.

VICKIE. On them?

SYLVIA. Ten per cent of their bar bill's on top of your basic. My best girl's commission tops twenty.

VICKIE. A month?

SYLVIA. A week.

VICKIE. Well, I never!

SYLVIA. Work hard and you'll get the rewards.

VICKIE. Oh, don't you worry, I will.

>   RUTH *rushes in with a scarf around her head.*

RUTH. Don't start, it's the smog.

SYLVIA. I got here in time.

RUTH. I had an appointment.

SYLVIA. Who with? The whole town's ground to a halt.

RUTH. Not Pierre!

>   RUTH *whips off the headscarf to reveal platinum blonde hair. There is a rapid-fire burst of camera flashes.*

SYLVIA. What's that?

RUTH. What do you think?

SYLVIA. Morrie likes you brunette.

RUTH. Well, Morrie can lump it. Gents prefer blondes, don't you know?

VICKIE. Afternoon.

SYLVIA. Ruth, Valerie. Valerie, Ruth.

RUTH. New char?

SYLVIA. New hostess.

RUTH. With a crop?

VICKIE. Chignon.

SYLVIA. Natural look, ain't it?

RUTH. Natural for boys.

SYLVIA. Continental.

RUTH (*taps her hair*). Hollywood.

VICKIE. Burns your head, don't it? Peroxide.

RUTH. Well, beauty is pain.

VICKIE. I'll say. I know a girl bleached her hair. Woke up bald as a coot.

RUTH. Camera Club?

VICKIE. Click-click.

RUTH. And what do you think of it?

VICKIE. Not bad at first but I'm bored of it now.

RUTH. And it's winter. Who wants stalac-tits, eh?

   RUTH *winks at* VICKIE, *who laughs*.

SYLVIA. And when you've quite finished…?

RUTH. Yes, dear?

SYLVIA. Who did you have in last night?

RUTH. Racing crowd.

SYLVIA. Drive a car through, did they?

RUTH. There was a small altercation.

SYLVIA. You don't say?

RUTH. Some fella got hold of the siphon.

SYLVIA. Again?

RUTH. Soaked Mike Hawthorn with soda, then only shoved ice down his neck.

SYLVIA. Silly boy.

RUTH. Mike throws a punch, cracks poor old Cliff Davis instead. His specs go flying, Cliff thumps him back, Sterling gets stuck in –

SYLVIA. The Court Club's select or have they forgot?

RUTH. Forgotten, dear.

VICKIE. Why didn't you chuck 'em all out?

RUTH. In the smog? We'd have lost 'em for ever.

SYLVIA. Good riddance, I say.

RUTH. You won't when when you open the safe.

SYLVIA. Oh?

RUTH. We only took eighty-three pounds.

VICKIE. How much?!

SYLVIA. Eighty-three?

RUTH *taps her hair.*

RUTH. And a generous tip.

SYLVIA (*to* VICKIE). See? That's what you get if you put your back in.

RUTH. And put your back out upstairs.

VICKIE. Upstairs?

RUTH. Don't look like that, dear. You know how it is.

VICKIE. How what is exactly?

SYLVIA. Come on, Audrey Hepburn? Why do you think Morrie sent you?

VICKIE. To give me a helping hand.

RUTH. Quite. And that's what you'll be giving him back.

VICKIE. Oh?

SYLVIA. Morrie has keys to the doors.

VICKIE. Our doors?

SYLVIA. And some nights, he calls for his rent.

VICKIE. I see…

SYLVIA. As I said, there's a nice little dress shop next door. Nine-to-five, no strings attached.

VICKIE. I could do that in Staines. (*Corrects herself.*) Egham.

SYLVIA. Ambition ain't all it's cracked up to be, dear.

VICKIE. But I've got it, Miss Shaw. And I ain't going back.

RUTH. Not going back.

SYLVIA. Sylvia.

RUTH. Don't you worry, he doesn't take long.

VICKIE. Well, that much I know from last night.

RUTH laughs.

SYLVIA. I'll keep an eye on you, dear.

RUTH turns up the gramophone for the middle-eighth of 'Love for Sale' and offers VICKIE her hand.

RUTH. Just stay on your twinkle-toes, eh? Shall we?

In a mirrorball light, RUTH and VICKIE dance and discover one another. Laughing, they change leads, performing for each other and dazzling whoever is watching, especially GALE.

GALE. If London's a market, then this is the trading floor. Black tie and bullet bra. Gentlemen, girls-on-the-make: buying and selling; bonds and securities; gold mines and diamonds and cash. The real Stock Exchange. Sit here, you'll soon see who's rising, who's falling, who's lost it all, who's made a killing.

The record sticks, leaving a static trail in the air.

SYLVIA. What more can I tell you? They're ordinary girls.

GALE. I'd say they're anything but.

Scene Five

Six camera flashes, fired in an irregular pattern. SYLVIA *tops up* GALE's *glass.*

As she does, RUTH *sits down with a pile of napkins to fold. She sings 'Love for Sale' to herself.* VICKIE *is declaiming from a well-thumbed script.*

VICKIE. 'Talk about the glamorous life of a mannequin. In this dump, all the clothes are designed to look like a maiden aunt.'

RUTH. So who else is in it?

VICKIE. Jane Hylton.

RUTH. Jane Hylton? She's terribly plain.

VICKIE. No, she ain't.

RUTH. Isn't.

VICKIE. You've not even met her.

RUTH. Have you?

VICKIE. Not today but she'll be in my scene.

RUTH. That's not her real name, you know? She used to be Gwendolene Clark.

VICKIE. Gwendolene? Sounds like a cough mixture.

RUTH. Time for your Gwendolene, dear.

VICKIE (*laughs*). I'm changing my name, an' all.

RUTH. To what?

VICKIE. Vickie Martin.

RUTH. And who dreamed that up?

VICKIE. Stephen.

RUTH. Our own Henry Higgins.

VICKIE. No more cleaning ashtrays and dirty old men at the door. No, it's lights, camera, action for me!

RUTH *takes the script from* VICKIE.

RUTH. What's it called, then? The film.

VICKIE. *It Started in Paradise*.

RUTH. Ended in tears.

VICKIE. It's set in a fashion salon. West End. Madame Alìce, she's a *grande dame* –

RUTH. Played by?

VICKIE. Martita Hunt.

RUTH. She's Miss Havisham, *Great Expectations*.

VICKIE. You could have played her part.

RUTH. What do you mean?

VICKIE. She's an old bat in this one, an' all.

RUTH. I'll give you an old bat… round the head.

RUTH *rolls up the script to swipe* VICKIE.

VICKIE. Watch it, that's got to go back.

RUTH. Who to?

VICKIE. Some girl with three lines who'd gone to the ladies'.

RUTH. You pinched it?

VICKIE. One has to prepare. If Jane Hylton falls ill…

RUTH. Or Martita…

RUTH *unrolls the script*.

VICKIE (*laughing*). Go on.

VICKIE *prompts* RUTH *to read Madame Alìce*.

RUTH. 'What's gone wrong? What's happened to me? My clients used to rely on me absolutely.'

VICKIE. Next!

RUTH. 'Why, not one of them would buy a pair of gloves without asking my advice. The Duchess of Derbyshire, for instance.'

RUTH *prompts* VICKIE *to read with her.*

VICKIE. 'The Duchess of Derbyshire?'

RUTH. 'Not this one, the last one. I remember the Grand Duchess Natalie saying to me: "You have the best taste in Europe – dress me." And I made everything she wore.'

VICKIE. 'What became of the Grand Duchess?'

RUTH. 'She was killed… in a revolution.'

VICKIE. Don't give up the day job.

RUTH. I've made a film, actually.

VICKIE. Oh? *Blink and You'll Miss Me*, weren't it?

RUTH. *Lady Godiva Rides Again.*

VICKIE. At a fleapit near you.

RUTH. With Diana Dors.

VICKIE. Fluck.

RUTH. Same to you.

VICKIE. Her real name's Fluck.

RUTH. I know that, she's a friend. A good friend.

VICKIE. Funny she don't drop in?

RUTH. Doesn't.

VICKIE. Exactly.

RUTH. She knows you're here, Calamity Jane.

VICKIE *takes the script and defiantly flicks it open.*

VICKIE. Excuse me? 'Third Model.'

RUTH. Third?

VICKIE. Third as in 'best comes last'.

RUTH. Third but no name?

VICKIE *returns to the script.*

VICKIE. In my 'beach ensemble of turquoise-blue cotton, trimmed with white. Third Model removes skirt to reveal puffball shorts.'

RUTH. Puffball?

VICKIE. It's Old English-style, ain't it? 'Walks side to side – '

RUTH. Like an old English crab?

VICKIE *elegantly enacts her moves.*

VICKIE. 'Walks side to side. Removes top to reveal bikini.'

RUTH. Removes bikini to reveal…

VICKIE. That's your sort of film, dear.

RUTH. And don't raise your hopes. Girls can end up on the cutting-room floor.

VICKIE. With the director? Given half a chance.

SYLVIA *steps into the scene.*

SYLVIA. Cutting room? What about my floor, it's filthy.

VICKIE. Get to it, then.

SYLVIA. You work here, don't you?

VICKIE. For now.

RUTH. Val –

VICKIE. Vickie!

SYLVIA. I told you to do it last night.

VICKIE. And put the poor char out of work?

SYLVIA. What char?

VICKIE. Not again?

RUTH. What happened to this one?

SYLVIA. She's gone to pick strawberries in Kent.

VICKIE. Let's hope they choke her.

SYLVIA *whips the script away from* VICKIE.

SYLVIA. You're paid to look pretty, dear, not learn your words on my time.

VICKIE. I don't have none.

RUTH. Thank heavens.

VICKIE. I say it all with a look.

VICKIE *shows* SYLVIA *her look*.

RUTH. Not bad for a girl from Staines.

VICKIE. Egham.

SYLVIA. Who's showed you that, then?

RUTH. Who do you think? Stephen Ward.

SYLVIA. Oh, aye?

VICKIE. He says I've got it.

SYLVIA. And he'd know, being a doctor.

VICKIE. An osteopath.

SYLVIA. Whatever that is.

VICKIE. He's treated Gandhi – and Churchill.

RUTH. He has, I've seen the photos.

VICKIE. He gave me a back rub, an' all. Same hands what's touched greatness.

SYLVIA. I've heard they've been everywhere.

VICKIE. He opens doors, Sylvie. With gold-plated handles.

RUTH. And knockers.

VICKIE (*laughs*). Knockers?

RUTH. You do have a filthy mind, dear.

VICKIE *and* RUTH *are now supressing a fit of the giggles.*

SYLVIA. Napkins. Floor.

SYLVIA *returns to the bar with the script.*

VICKIE. Sylvie? My script.

SYLVIA. It's going straight on the fire.

VICKIE. She wouldn't?

RUTH. She won't.

VICKIE. She'll put up my picture here one day, you wait. She'll have a plaque on the wall.

RUTH. 'Here Lived Valerie Mewes.'

VICKIE. 'Vickie Martin. Hostess and Hollywood star.'

RUTH. 'Here Lived Ruth Ellis.'

VICKIE. 'The Best Lay in London.'

RUTH. I beg your pardon?

VICKIE. That's what he said, ain't it? That's what I heard through the wall.

RUTH. Well, you shouldn't have been listening.

VICKIE. I didn't have a choice. (*Teasing her.*) 'Oh, David!'

RUTH. You didn't hear that.

VICKIE. You called him a pompous ass last week.

RUTH. He is but I took him down.

VICKIE. I know you did, dear.

RUTH. And up close, he's…

VICKIE. What?

RUTH. He's got lovely long eyelashes.

VICKIE. Haven't we all?

RUTH. He's almost like one of the Lost Boys.

VICKIE. Oh?

RUTH. He fell out of his pram in Kensington Gardens and nobody noticed he'd gone.

VICKIE. And you're Wendy?

RUTH. I'm nothing. It's done now. We're ships in the night.

VICKIE. What if he comes sailing back?

RUTH. He's engaged.

VICKIE. You're married. You still wear the ring.

RUTH. It's my bad hand, it's stuck on the joint.

VICKIE. Let's have a look.

   VICKIE *tries to pull the ring off.*

RUTH. Careful!

VICKIE. Still hurts?

RUTH. Always will but worse happens at sea.

VICIKIE. Factory work, eh?

RUTH. Three pound a week and rheumatic fever.

VICKIE. It got you out, though.

RUTH. It did. I was lucky.

VICKIE. Deformed but lucky.

RUTH. Excuse me? That's deform-ation of character.

   VICKIE *adopts a Dr Frankenstein voice.*

VICKIE. Knockers.

RUTH. Knockers to you, too.

   RUTH *puts her hands to* VICKIE*'s throat, mugging like a silent-film star.*

VICKIE. 'What became of the Grand Duchess?'

Bathed in a flickering projector light, they play out a Hollywood dream.

RUTH. 'She was killed… in a –

VICKIE *and* RUTH. – Revolution!'

GALE and SYLVIA are caught in the projector light. The spool click-clicks beneath RUTH and VICKIE's laughter.

GALE. Shapes start to swirl in the static. Feelings are given a form. In the dead of the night comes a vision so clear… you turn on the light and she's…

The projector spools out, leaving GALE and SYLVIA in the morning light, with no trace of VICKIE and RUTH. SYLVIA nods to GALE and he exits.

Scene Six

From the static comes 'Good Morning Heartache' by Billie Holiday. DORIS JUDD turns up the gramophone as far as she dares. She sings a few bars, losing herself in the music. She doesn't see SYLVIA come into the club.

SYLVIA. Worker's playtime, is it?

DORIS. Beg your pardon, Miss Shaw. I didn't know you was here.

SYLVIA. I slept upstairs last night.

SYLVIA turns the gramophone down.

DORIS. Beg your pardon.

SYLVIA. Don't apologise, dear. Not for her.

DORIS. She helps you along, don't she?

SYLVIA. I'll say.

DORIS. In all sorts of ways.

SYLVIA. And we need all the help we can get.

DORIS. Yes, Miss Shaw.

DORIS *turns the gramophone back up a little and returns to work.* SYLVIA *finds an egg and cracks it into a glass, mixes it with Worcestershire Sauce and drinks it in one. As she puts the glass down,* DORIS *is watching her.*

SYLVIA. Something I ate.

DORIS. Fish? My fella says he was sick as a dog once on fish.

SYLVIA. You've got a fella?

DORIS. Yes, miss. It was coley, I think.

SYLVIA. Since when?

DORIS. Three weeks ago at a dance.

SYLVIA. Well…

DORIS. I know.

SYLVIA. Courting.

DORIS. Who'd have thought?

SYLVIA. Just as long as it don't interfere with your job.

DORIS. Oh, it won't do, Miss Shaw.

SYLVIA. You're a good little worker. Your standards are higher than mine.

DORIS. I do my best for you, miss. I do.

SYLVIA. And God loves a trier, so you keep it up, dear, all right?

SYLVIA *goes to leave but* DORIS *speaks up.*

DORIS. Oh, you can be sure of it, miss. Now I'm engaged to be married.

SYLVIA. Engaged?

DORIS. Since last Sunday. Half-four, Clapham Common.

SYLVIA. That's a bit hasty, ain't it?

DORIS. We don't think so.

SYLVIA. Not up the duff, are you?

DORIS. No, miss!

SYLVIA. You sure?

DORIS (*voice rising*). I can tell you with certainty –

SYLVIA. All right, all right!

   SYLVIA *touches her temple*.

DORIS. He's a young man who knows his own mind.

SYLVIA. I'll say.

DORIS. He's a plumber's apprentice. Plays the piano but d'you
   know what? He's never had a lesson in his life.

SYLVIA. Well, well.

DORIS. He's a gift for it, see?

SYLVIA. Good.

DORIS. And I sing along.

SYLVIA. Ain' that nice?

   SYLVIA *turns to go but* DORIS *sings a few lines of 'God
   Bless the Child'*.

   Nice.

DORIS. 'Tis, miss. It feels like you're floating on air.

SYLVIA. Well, don't you float off when you're Mrs…

DORIS. Arkwright, and there's no chance of that.

SYLVIA. Good.

DORIS. This is the finest position I've had.

SYLVIA. Life's on the up, then.

DORIS. And we'll be saving, of course, for a place of our own.

SYLVIA. Good for you.

DORIS. So if you've additional duties, Miss Shaw? Laundry, deliveries... what's due this morning, spirits and wine?

SYLVIA. If it's Wednesday.

DORIS. It is, miss. My favourite day.

SYLVIA. Oh?

DORIS. Halfway through, ain't it? Worst's over, the best yet to come.

Beat.

SYLVIA. You stay for the drayman. I'm going back to bed.

DORIS. Thank you, Miss Shaw.

SYLVIA. Keep a note of your hours in the book.

DORIS. And, miss? I could perform a little, perhaps?

SYLVIA. Perform?

DORIS. At night for the gentlemen.

SYLVIA. You?

DORIS. And my Albert. You don't have to pay us. We'd put a dish on the piano, that's all, and see what the gentlemen –

SYLVIA. No!

RUTH *comes in with a suitcase. She moves slowly, as if she might break.*

RUTH. Oh, Sylvie, give her a go.

SYLVIA. What are you doing here?

RUTH. I'd heard talk you missed me.

RUTH *feels a pain in her abdomen.* DORIS *steps forward.*

DORIS. Mrs Ellis...

RUTH. It's the taxi, that's all.

DORIS. Take my arm.

RUTH. Driver hit every bump in the road.

DORIS. Steady now.

RUTH glances at DORIS as she helps her to her seat.

RUTH. You're still here?

DORIS. Why wouldn't I be, Mrs Ellis?

RUTH. How long is it now?

DORIS. Six weeks.

RUTH (*to* SYLVIA). That must be a record?

SYLVIA. Why didn't you say you were coming?

RUTH. I didn't know I was till I was.

RUTH lowers herself carefully into a seat.

DORIS. Careful.

RUTH. I'm all right. It's only the stitches are sore.

SYLVIA. Sore? What doctor's discharged you like this?

RUTH. They didn't. I left.

SYLVIA. Six weeks of bed-rest, they said.

RUTH. And that's what I'll have. In my own bed, with my own things around me.

SYLVIA. Well, make sure the curtains are closed.

RUTH. Don't start, you look worse than me.

Beat.

SYLVIA. Long night.

RUTH. Who with?

SYLVIA. That's my business and don't think I'm nursing you here.

RUTH. You don't have to.

SYLVIA. I mean it. I don't do ablutions or dressings.

RUTH. I'll do them.

RUTH takes a pillbox from her handbag.

DORIS. I'll do them, if need be. I cared for my auntie with ulcers, you've never seen anything like 'em, they're open and –

SYLVIA. Yes, thank you, Doris.

RUTH. And I'm on the mend. The infection's all gone. It's just a bit tender, that's all.

SYLVIA. So what's them?

RUTH. Scotch mist.

SYLVIA. Painkillers?

RUTH. And one for my nerves.

SYLVIA. I didn't know you had nerves?

RUTH. I won't in a bit.

RUTH *tries to get up.*

SYLVIA. Ruth!

DORIS. Now what is it?

RUTH. Can I trouble you for water?

SYLVIA. Doris? Pot of tea, please.

DORIS. Strong and sweet, miss. A steadying brew for us all.

DORIS *goes into the kitchen, watched by* RUTH.

RUTH. Strong and sweet.

'Good Morning Heartache' fades up.

RUTH *opens her compact and powders her face.* SYLVIA *goes to the drinks cabinet and pours two glasses of brandy.*

GALE *comes in with a document and reads.*

GALE. 'Rheumatic fever, aged fifteen.

Tubal pregnancy.

Two abortions.'

SYLVIA. Well, that's how it goes.

GALE. 'Good health except for a genital infection of a non-venereal type. Had treatment in custody.

Bruise upon the left thigh, more recent bruise on the right forearm.'

SYLVIA. She fell. Probably.

RUTH *takes off her spectacles to powder under her eyes.*

GALE. 'Only defect of central nervous system a minor defect of vision corrected by spectacles.'

RUTH *puts her spectacles back on and gazes at her reflection.*

SYLVIA. Blind as a bat. Especially where blokes are concerned.

GALE. 'No evidence of mental disease.'

RUTH *snaps the compact shut.*

SYLVIA. No.

GALE. 'With regard to her alleged offence, there is no suggestion she was under the influence of drugs or alcohol.'

SYLVIA *picks up the brandy glasses and returns to* RUTH *without a backward glance to* GALE.

Miss Shaw?

Scene Seven

Continuous action. SYLVIA *gives* RUTH *a glass of brandy and drinks one herself.* GALE *remains, studying his paperwork.*

SYLVIA. You need your bumps read.

RUTH. I'm sorry?

SYLVIA. You need your head testing, gal.

RUTH. Oh, they did at the hospital. (*Knocks her head with her knuckles.*) No, nothing there.

SYLVIA. A tubal can do for you.

RUTH. Nine lives, that's me.

SYLVIA. Why don't you take some precautions?

RUTH. Can't, I'm a good Catholic girl.

SYLVIA. The Pope washed his hands of you long ago. Tell 'em to bag it up.

RUTH. Some men don't like to. Well, not with me.

SYLVIA. They don't 'like to' with anyone.

RUTH. I'm different.

SYLVIA. How so?

RUTH. And I can take care of myself.

RUTH *takes the tablets, washed down with the brandy.*

SYLVIA. So who was it this time?

RUTH. A regular.

SYLVIA. Blakely?

RUTH. That's finished.

SYLVIA. Again?

RUTH. Has he asked about me?

SYLVIA. Not especially.

RUTH. He hasn't?

SYLVIA. I didn't say that.

RUTH. Well, has he or not?

SYLVIA. I don't make small talk with overgrown schoolboys.

RUTH. Why? What's he done? Who's he been with?

SYLVIA. That's not your concern.

RUTH. Yes, it is!

SYLVIA. Oi! Hold your tongue.

RUTH. Who's he been with while I've been away?

SYLVIA. Oh, so that's why you're back? To check up on loverboy?

RUTH. No.

SYLVIA. Pull the other one, Ruth.

Beat.

RUTH. Hasn't he?

Beat.

SYLVIA. I'll tell you who has. Desmond Cussen.

RUTH. Desmond...

SYLVIA. Cussen. He follows the racing crowd. Quite an admirer, he is.

RUTH. Of me?

SYLVIA. Enquired of you only last night.

RUTH. Where did you tell him I was?

SYLVIA. Visiting friends in the country.

RUTH. Some friends.

SYLVIA. Don't look like that, dear. You're going straight back. Morrie's paid for a bed for six weeks –

RUTH. I don't care, I can't.

SYLVIA. You can if he tells you to.

RUTH. No! I've spent enough time in those sorts of… no.

DORIS *brings a tray with a teapot, milk jug, sugar and two cups.*

DORIS. Tea for two.

DORIS *pours the tea.*

RUTH. They sent me away to have Andy. Great draughty house with damp bedding. Mother said: 'Don't bring him back here,' but why wouldn't I? We were going to get married.

DORIS. Who?

SYLVIA. Just pour the tea, dear.

DORIS *sugars the tea.*

RUTH. If he hadn't been killed in the war.

DORIS. Mrs Ellis?

RUTH *takes the teacup with a trembling hand.*

SYLVIA. Dear God.

RUTH. It's my bad hand, that's all.

DORIS. Let me…

DORIS *takes* RUTH*'s cup, puts it down.*

RUTH. It's the brandy… goes straight to your head.

DORIS. But you're all right. You're home now. You're home.

SYLVIA. Seen Vickie, have you?

RUTH. In the *Daily Express*. At a party with Diana Dors.

SYLVIA. Did she pay you a visit, I mean?

RUTH. Once, on the way out to Cliveden. Some chap was outside in the car. Click, clack, click, clack in her heels up the ward like she's on the catwalk.

SYLVIA. Did she tell you she's gone?

RUTH. Gone?

DORIS. She left.

SYLVIA. Weeks ago.

RUTH. Where to?

SYLVIA. Belgravia.

RUTH. She never said.

SYLVIA. And don't ask us who's paying the rent.

DORIS. She's in with Lord So-and-So, ain't she?

RUTH. Belgravia... who'd have thought... well...

DORIS *puts the back of her hand against* RUTH's *forehead.*

SYLVIA. Is she burning up?

DORIS. Yes.

SYLVIA. Right, I'm phoning an ambulance.

RUTH. No, please! Just put me to bed.

SYLVIA. Four flights up? You'll be dead on arrival.

DORIS. I'll take her.

RUTH. I'm sure I can manage.

DORIS. I'll stay. Miss Shaw?

Beat.

SYLVIA. Do you think you can get her right? Properly right, so she's ready to...

RUTH. What?

Beat.

SYLVIA. Morrie's got plans for you.

RUTH. What sort of plans?

SYLVIA. A position's come up. Brompton Road. Used to be Dorothy's, now it's The Little.

RUTH. Ten gents up there makes it a party.

SYLVIA. So what do you reckon?

RUTH. About what?

SYLVIA. Vickie's gone and there's new girls come in. We think it'll suit you.

RUTH. I see.

RUTH's eyes are full.

SYLVIA. Now what?

RUTH. I'm damaged goods, aren't I? Too old and spent for The Court.

SYLVIA. Not to work it, you silly… To run it.

RUTH. Run it?

SYLVIA. When you're back on your feet.

RUTH. But I'm not a manageress.

SYLVIA. Why not? You've earned your stripes here. And what you're not sure of, I'd show you.

RUTH. I can't…

SYLVIA. Morrie's doing it up. Be ready the same time as you are, I'd say. There's a flat there, two bedrooms. One for you, one for Andy. Get him back from your ma's, ain't that what you want?

RUTH. He'd allow me to have him?

SYLVIA. I'll make sure he does.

Beat.

RUTH. How much would I have to turn over?

SYLVIA. Less than a thousand a month. And he'd start you on fifteen a week. Ten pound entertainment allowance on top, plus commission.

RUTH. Brompton Road's Knightsbridge...

SYLVIA. Means knuckling down, mind. No more of this trouble, do you hear me? No more.

RUTH. Yes. No. No more.

SYLVIA. I'd be counting on you.

RUTH. Course.

SYLVIA. You'd need to step up, Ruth. Command the respect of your girls.

DORIS. You could do that, I know it.

SYLVIA. I told you the first day you came here: you work hard, you get the rewards.

RUTH. The Little Club...

SYLVIA. Is that a yes?

RUTH. But how will you manage without me?

DORIS. It's all right, Mrs Ellis. I'm here.

SYLVIA *puts a record on the gramophone: 'Nice Work if You Can Get It' by Billie Holiday.*

Scene Eight

As the song plays, DORIS *assists* RUTH *in changing clothes, shoes, hair and accessories, preparing her for her new role. The* COMPANY *set up the club.*

GALE. The Little Club…

SYLVIA. Three flights up. Can't swing a cat but it swings.

GALE. With whom?

SYLVIA. Peers of the realm; lonely ex-servicemen; junior doctors; ministers –

GALE. Church or State?

SYLVIA. Both.

GALE. Blakely followed her there?

SYLVIA. Yep. And Cussen.

GALE *flips open his pocketbook and reads his notes.*

GALE. Desmond Cussen. Company Director. Ex-Air Force, impeccable record.

SYLVIA. On paper.

Only when RUTH *is ready does* DORIS *take off her overall and fix her own hair.*

GALE. Oh?

SYLVIA. Last drink, all right? I've said enough.

GALE *sits at the bar and takes a drink. As he does,* VICKIE *enters and a flashbulb explodes six times, in an irregular pattern.*

Scene Nine

GALE *settles in a shadowy corner.* DORIS *clears up and* VICKIE *helps herself to a drink. Her leg is bandaged.*

VICKIE. And I say she should be admired.

DORIS. I'm sure.

VICKIE. Instead of denying it, what does she do? (*As Marilyn.*) 'I posed nude for the money. And I looked beautiful, too.'

DORIS. Excuse me.

DORIS *cleans up around* VICKIE.

VICKIE. She was selling her assets. So that's what I'll say when my Camera Club pictures come out. 'I'm a modern girl, too.'

DORIS. We know that, Miss Martin.

VICKIE *gestures to her drink.*

VICKIE. She won't mind me helping myself. We share everything.

DORIS. Do you?

VICKIE. I'll go up, shall I?

VICKIE *doesn't wait for an answer.*

DORIS. We're closed.

VICKIE. I'm not a customer, dear.

VICKIE *moves as if to go upstairs.*

DORIS. What have you done to your leg?

VICKIE *does a Marilyn turn.*

VICKIE. Oh, you don't read the papers?

DORIS. Not the society page.

VICKIE. You should if you work here.

DORIS. I don't, as it happens. I char for Miss Shaw and help out.

VICKIE. Well, we'd been to the races, my fella and I. Drunk Pimm's, had a marvellous time. I said: 'Put your foot down, my dear. It's a sports car, ain't it?' Silly boy takes a corner too fast. Hits the kerb, flips us into a ditch. Splat!

DORIS. You could have been killed.

VICKIE. Not me, I'm a rubber ball. Bouncy-bounce.

DORIS. And your gentleman… Coochie?

VICKIE. You do read the papers!

DORIS. Mrs Ellis showed me a cutting.

VICKIE. He gets everso cross if you call him that.

DORIS. Was he hurt worse than you, Miss?

VICKIE. Five broken ribs and a collarbone.

DORIS. Ouch.

VICKIE. His real name's Bhayai. Prince Bhayai. His Highness Sri Sri Maharaja Jagaddipendra Narayan Bhup Bahadur, Maharaja of Cooch-Behar.

DORIS. My chap's called Bert.

VICKIE. I'll be a Maharani, of course. When we marry.

DORIS. I'll be a Mrs.

VICKIE. He proposes to me every Friday… with bouquets of flowers you couldn't even name.

DORIS. Indians marry their own, don't they? Cos of religion, an' that?

VICKIE. Oh, we'll do it clandestine. That's much more romantic than church.

DORIS. Not to me.

VICKIE *looks at* DORIS.

VICKIE. You're a funny thing, aren't you? For a hostess?

DORIS. I've told you, I'm not. I'm the help.

VICKIE. And does she need help – Ruth?

DORIS. Sometimes. With Andy, you know?

VICKIE. How old is he now?

DORIS. Nine.

VICKIE. What kind of kid is he these days?

DORIS. He's curious.

VICKIE. Eager or odd?

DORIS. He goes to museums on his own.

VICKIE. Odd.

DORIS. I sit with him. Read him a story. And when he's asleep, I come down.

VICKIE. And what does your fella say? Nice girl like you working here?

DORIS. For the last time, I don't.

VICKIE. Ain't he concerned?

DORIS. About what?

VICKIE. All the trouble you have?

DORIS. Trouble?

VICKIE. You know what I mean.

DORIS. Do I?

VICKIE. Word gets around.

DORIS. From Miss Shaw? I told her in confidence.

VICKIE. Told her what?

Beat.

DORIS. I'd rather not say.

VICKIE. Doris?

DORIS. I ain't a gossip.

VICKIE. And I ain't a fool. What?

Beat.

DORIS. I was crossing the floor with a trayful of glasses to wash. A man sees me coming, puts out his foot, trips me up.

VICKIE. Which man? Blakely?

DORIS. I'm flat on the floor and he's laughing. I pick myself up, brush myself down, bite my lip... and then...

VICKIE. What?

DORIS. I see the siphon, right there on the bar. And something came over me, I don't know what. So I pick it up, turn around, wipe the smirk off his face.

VICKIE. Good job it wasn't a gun.

DORIS. Mrs Ellis runs upstairs, he follows her.

VICKIE. Face dripping wet.

DORIS. He's ranting and raving: 'Get rid of her, now.' Something gets smashed and all I can think of is Andy.

VICKIE. He must be used to it now.

DORIS. And all of a sudden, it goes deathly quiet. I creep upstairs. Wait on the landing. Knock-knock. No reply. What he's done to her, God only knows. I turn the handle, open the door, peep through and they're...

VICKIE. What?

DORIS. I can't say it.

VICKIE. In bed.

DORIS. After all that...

VICKIE. Bloody loverboy...

DORIS. He's living here now.

VICKIE. So I've heard.

DORIS. She gives him money, buys him clothes, pays for cigarettes. Takings are falling and what does he contribute? Nothing.

VICKIE. Still racing, is he?

DORIS. He's building a car.

VICKIE. Boys and their toys.

DORIS. It's running on gin from the bar.

VICKIE. That's why it don't get off the grid?

DORIS. I wish Mr Cussen would give him what for.

VICKIE. Mr Who?

DORIS. Cussen. Desmond.

VICKIE. That slimy bloke with the 'tache?

DORIS. He's a wholesale tobacconist.

VICKIE. He only comes up to here.

VICKIE *gestures his height on her arm.*

DORIS. But he stands when she enters the room. Finds her a chair, fills her glass, sends her lovely carnations –

VICKIE. She's screwing him, too?

DORIS. Don't say it like that.

VICKIE. Is she?

DORIS. It's possible, yes. To spite Mr Blakely, I suppose.

RUTH *appears in the shadows.*

VICKIE. But Desmond? She don't even like him.

DORIS. She does in a fatherly way.

VICKIE. And we know what her father is.

Beat.

DORIS. What?

VICKIE *gets up to leave.*

VICKIE. It's late.

DORIS. Miss Martin?

VICKIE. Tell her I called.

DORIS. I've spoke very open to you. If there's something you know that –

VICKIE. There's not.

DORIS. No?

Beat.

VICKIE. It's just once we were talking, that's all. And she started to say… we were sloshed, it was probably –

RUTH. We're shut.

RUTH *emerges from the darkness. She wears her spectacles and a man's dinner jacket over a nightdress. She has bare feet. She walks a blurred route to the drinks.*

VICKIE. Madame Alìce!

RUTH. What are you doing here?

VICKIE. I've been for dinner at Claridge's. Dear me, there's only so much you can take. Last drink at The Little, I thought.

RUTH *clumsily searches through the bottles.*

DORIS. So that's nice for you, ain't it? Miss Martin's come specially to –

RUTH. Where is it?

DORIS. What?

RUTH. Pernod.

DORIS. We're out.

RUTH. We can't be.

DORIS. You had the last bottle last night.

RUTH. We've another in stock, though?

DORIS. We've nothing in stock, Mrs Ellis.

RUTH. Well, don't look so worried. We've gin.

RUTH *takes a bottle of gin and heads back in the direction she came.*

VICKIE. Are you keeping it all to yourself?

RUTH. It's only a nightcap.

VICKIE. So have one with me.

RUTH. I can't.

VICKIE. Why?

RUTH. You know how it is.

VICKIE. Yes, I do, dear. And that's why I'm here.

RUTH *looks at* VICKIE.

RUTH. 'Night.

RUTH *turns to go.*

VICKIE. Last Tuesday, The Steering Wheel Club? Had a good time, did you?

RUTH. What do you mean?

VICKIE. What I say. You were there, weren't you?

Beat.

RUTH. No.

VICKIE. Oh? So you didn't see what went off?

RUTH. No.

DORIS. What?

VICKIE. A couple came in. All smiles, so I've heard. Then out of nowhere, a big row blew up and he gave her a punch in the face.

DORIS. In the club?

VICKIE. In clear view of everyone. Well, except Mrs Ellis, it seems.

RUTH. You shouldn't listen to gossip.

VICKIE. And you shouldn't take it, dear God!

RUTH. I don't, as it happens. I've hit him back, twice as hard. Scratched his face, pulled a knife on him once –

DORIS. You don't push him down stairs, Mrs Ellis.

RUTH. I fell.

DORIS. He ran down and stepped right over you.

RUTH. He wasn't himself.

DORIS. I was begging you: 'Don't let him back.' And you swore to me that –

RUTH. It's passion. That's all it is, passion.

VICKIE. It's pitiful.

> RUTH *looks at* VICKIE.

RUTH. I think you should leave now, dear.

VICKIE. Not without you.

RUTH. I'm asking you nicely, now: go.

VICKIE. And I'm asking you, Duchess –

RUTH (*explodes*). For Christ's sake, we're not Sylvie's girls any more!

DORIS. Mrs Ellis!

RUTH (*to* VICKIE). And you... you know nothing of me or my... nothing, all right?

> *Beat.*

VICKIE. Fine.

> VICKIE *goes to leave.*

DORIS. But, Miss Martin, you came here specially...

VICKIE. I know. Silly me. Keep the change.

> VICKIE *gives* DORIS *a pound note and leaves.* DORIS *offers the money to* RUTH.

DORIS. Here.

RUTH. Get a cab home.

DORIS. I don't want –

RUTH. Get a cab.

DORIS *puts the money aside*.

DORIS. Shall I come in tomorrow?

RUTH. If you like.

DORIS. Would you like?

RUTH. Of course. I can't do without you, can I?

GALE *steps out of the shadows, watching*.

DORIS. Mrs Ellis? What is it about him?

RUTH *is distracted by the shadowy figure*.

RUTH. It's what they call chemistry, dear.

DORIS. So was Hiroshima, ma'am.

DORIS *leaves, her eyes to the floor*.

Scene Ten

Dead of night.

GALE *comes into focus. He goes to the gramophone, flips the record over and places the needle onto it*.

GALE. Detection is a science.

Method, analysis, logic.

Objectivity.

Proof beyond reasonable doubt.

RUTH *looks towards him, peering through the static*.

It's also an art.

Intuition.

Perception.

Rapport.

RUTH *takes off the jacket. Her body is bruised.*

It's the desire for justice.

For truth.

And of course –

It's the thrill of the chase.

From the static comes 'My Man' by Billie Holiday. As it plays, RUTH *turns out the jacket pockets. She studies its secrets: cigarettes, matches and calling cards. She finds a wallet and pulls it apart. Scraps of paper spill out but no cash.*

GALE *moves around her, picking up scraps to examine.*

In the inside pocket, RUTH *finds and inhales a vial of amyl nitrate. She pulls out a packet of Durex. She hurls it away. She rips at the jacket as she did the packet, tearing its sleeves, collar and pockets.*

RUTH *tries to put the jacket back together.* GALE *moves as close to her as he dare to.*

RUTH *looks up at him.*

RUTH. David…

Six gunshots sound in an irregular pattern.

ACT TWO

Scene One

Late at night, GALE *puts a record on the gramophone, which is beside him on the floor. The first verse and chorus of 'Gloomy Sunday' by Billie Holiday plays.*

GALE *turns back to his open case-file, with papers, photographs and reference books spread across the floor. Among the papers are Billie Holiday album covers and a half-empty whisky bottle and glass.*

GALE *is dishevelled. His shirt sleeves are roughly rolled up, his tie discarded.*

Working at home in the electric-fire light, we see the shadow of exhaustion on his face.

GALE. Holloway Prison. Thirteenth of April, 1955. Two days after shooting her lover at point-blank range, Prisoner 9656 pens a letter to his mother.

She tells her, 'I shall die loving your son. And you should feel content that his death has been repaid.' Her hand remains steady, her nails blood-red. She's resigned to her fate but I'm not.

GALE *takes a swig of whisky and finds a newspaper cutting among his papers.*

Four months ago. Golders Green.

'Gloomy Sunday' continues.

Scene Two

SYLVIA *and* DORIS *appear in the twilight. Their black coats and hats are dusted with snow.* RUTH *is a pace behind them, taking a sly drink from a hip flask.*

As they come into focus, a news photographer's flashbulb marks six photographs.

The street has the strange hush that a heavy snowfall brings. The hush is punctuated by the sound of passing cars. The last of the snow is gently falling.

SYLVIA, DORIS *and* RUTH *walk over the case notes as if they too are covered in snow.* GALE *shadows* RUTH.

SYLVIA. That's that, then.

RUTH *catches a dusting of snow in her hand.*

RUTH. Ashes to ashes. Dust to dusted.

DORIS. The service was nice, don't you think?

SYLVIA. I'm not having a funeral.

RUTH. Well, not today.

SYLVIA. 'Sylvia lived life to the full.' Sod that, she just stayed up too late.

DORIS. Miss Shaw, there's people in mourning.

SYLVIA. More fool them.

DORIS. Miss Shaw!

SYLVIA. I don't grieve and I don't pray; never have, never will.

RUTH. She should have given the sermon.

SYLVIA. Who's she, the cat's mother?

RUTH. 'Where, O death, is your victory? Where is your miaow?'

SYLVIA. Where's a bloody black cab when you want one?

DORIS. The weather, ain't it?

RUTH. So what happens now?

DORIS. We head back to The Court.

RUTH. No, to her.

   Beat.

DORIS. Well, they'll take her to Egham, I suppose.

RUTH. Staines.

SYLVIA. And we'll send her off with a glass of champagne.

RUTH. She said she'd go home in a silver Rolls Royce.

   RUTH *takes a swig from her hip flask.*

DORIS. Mrs Ellis...

RUTH. It's just to keep warm.

   RUTH *offers the hip flask to* DORIS.

DORIS. No.

RUTH. Just a tot?

DORIS. I said no.

RUTH. Nice word, isn't it? Tot. Tot, tot, tot, tot, tot, tot –

DORIS. Tell you what? Let's catch a bus.

SYLVIA. A bus?

RUTH. Big and red, dear.

SYLVIA. I'd rather get frostbite. (*Shouts.*) Taxi!

RUTH (*shying away*). Oh.

DORIS. Not so harshly! She's fragile.

SYLVIA. You baby her.

DORIS. You barely speak to her.

SYLVIA. Look at her. What's there to say?

DORIS. You might not be grieving, but she is.

SYLVIA. Is that what you call it?

DORIS. She's been in a world of her own since –

SYLVIA. She can stay there. At least she's not pestering me.

RUTH *is peering at* GALE*'s papers, not quite understanding what she is seeing.*

RUTH. Do you think perhaps they're wrong?

DORIS. Who?

RUTH. The papers. The doctors. The police.

DORIS. Not this time.

RUTH. They could be. I mean, lots of girls go to Cliveden. They could have confused her with...

SYLVIA. Who?

RUTH. But she never leaves early. She stays at a party till dawn.

SYLVIA. Not this time.

RUTH. But if she was so badly mangled, then how did they know it was her?

SYLVIA. Keep your voice down.

DORIS. And stay close, there's cameras.

RUTH. Where was Coochie? Why wasn't he there? I mean, what was she doing in a car with... who was it?

DORIS. A journalist.

SYLVIA. Same as she did every Sat'day.

RUTH. And how many spills has she had?

DORIS. Thirteen, the *Mirror* said.

RUTH. Thirteen, see? She walks away, that's what she does, silly cow. Walks away.

SYLVIA. Well, this time she didn't.

RUTH *twirls for the photographers.*

RUTH. Take my picture instead.

DORIS. Mrs Ellis.

RUTH. Come on, take it!

DORIS. Come away.

DORIS *takes hold of* RUTH, *who is laughing now.*

RUTH. And you know what's funny? I didn't even like her that much.

DORIS. Course you did.

RUTH. I didn't. She got on my wick. She said we were friends, then she dropped me for Diana Dors.

DORIS. That was just for the press.

RUTH. I'll say it was. Where are you now, dear Diana? Not at Golders Green Crem on a January day...

RUTH *takes another swig of her hip flask.*

DORIS. You've had enough now.

RUTH (*as* VICKIE). Not like her true pals who ain't gonna miss her at all.

DORIS. Why don't you –

RUTH. Stupid cow.

DORIS *tries to take the hip flask from* RUTH.

DORIS. Why don't you give it to me?

RUTH. Stupid, stupid, stupid –

SYLVIA. Ain't she on happy pills?

DORIS. Yes.

SYLVIA. Well, give her another.

RUTH. Stupid, stupid, stupid –

DORIS. Mrs Ellis?

SYLVIA. Ruth!

SYLVIA's 'Ruth' comes like a sobering slap in the face.

RUTH. Yes, Sylvie?

SYLVIA. Give the hip flask to Doris.

DORIS gently prises the hip flask from RUTH's grip.

DORIS. You don't want Desmond to see you like this, do you?

RUTH. He understands.

DORIS. Nor poor little Andy.

RUTH. Poor nothing, he's perfectly fine.

Beat.

SYLVIA. Nice flat he's got, has he? Cussen?

RUTH. Yes.

SYLVIA. It's better for Andy there? Better for you?

RUTH. Desmond provides.

SYLVIA. So you don't want to cause any trouble then, eh? You just want to keep it all nice.

RUTH. I am. I'm getting new photographs done.

SYLVIA. What kind of photographs?

RUTH. That's my business.

SYLVIA. And you're mine.

RUTH. Not since you sacked me.

SYLVIA. I didn't. Morrie decided –

RUTH. But you could have helped me.

SYLVIA. I got you set up, didn't I? And you've let me down, my dear. Badly.

DORIS. We all make mistakes –

RUTH. And when I start modelling again –

SYLVIA. What kind of modelling? Camera Club.

RUTH. When The Emperor takes off…

SYLVIA. The who?

RUTH. David's building a racing car.

SYLVIA. Still?

RUTH. With Findlater.

DORIS. Oh, Mrs Ellis.

RUTH. That's what they call it, The Emperor.

SYLVIA. More like The Emperor's New Clothes.

RUTH. It's different now, actually.

SYLVIA. How?

DORIS. You promised you'd stay right away.

RUTH. We're getting married.

SYLVIA. Really?

DORIS. You're what?

RUTH. He's proposed to me… properly, this time.

DORIS. When?

RUTH. Last night in The Rodney Hotel.

DORIS. Last night?

SYLVIA. I can't see a ring.

DORIS. When I've told you and told you…

RUTH. I have to go.

DORIS. No, you don't!

RUTH. Yes, I do, or he'll turn to that old married bitch or his
    cheap usherette or the Findlater's nanny, who's fat by the way.

SYLVIA *takes* RUTH *by the arm.*

SYLVIA. Right, miss. Let's take a walk to the Tube.

RUTH. In these shoes?

SYLVIA. It'll sober you up.

RUTH. No.

SYLVIA. Just do as you're –

RUTH. No!

SYLVIA. Do you want a good hiding, is that it?

DORIS. Not here!

SYLVIA. Cos by crikey, you're heading for one.

DORIS. Show some decorum, the pair of you. Please!

Beat.

SYLVIA. You had a chance, Ruth. Your one chance to raise
    yourself up –

RUTH. And I have. It's not an ordinary love affair. We're on a
    much higher plane.

SYLVIA. Dear God...

RUTH. He can't live without me. If I go, he'll kill himself,
    that's what he says.

SYLVIA. No, he won't.

RUTH. You don't know that.

SYLVIA. I do.

RUTH. How exactly?

SYLVIA. Because I had a father come back from the Somme,
    so don't talk to me about... don't.

Beat.

DORIS. Can we please just go home?

RUTH. In a silver Rolls Royce.

DORIS. Back to the club, miss? For champagne and...

SYLVIA. Taxi!

SYLVIA *hails an oncoming taxi.*

RUTH. I can't. I've made plans.

RUTH *is foraging in her handbag.*

DORIS. Who with?

RUTH. Desmond.

DORIS. Oh, good.

SYLVIA. Hallelujah, he's stopped.

RUTH. We're driving to Penn.

DORIS. Penn? Ain't that where loverboy's from?

RUTH. And the woman he screws. We'll find the slut and we'll see what she says when she knows about me and where is it, where is it, where is it?!

RUTH *wrenches open the handbag, drops it and the contents spill out.*

DORIS. It's all right, Mrs Ellis.

RUTH. My compact.

DORIS. No harm done.

DORIS *goes to pick them up.*

SYLVIA. Leave it.

DORIS. No harm.

SYLVIA. Let her do it herself.

DORIS. Are you blind, deaf and dumb now? She can't.

RUTH *pulls her compact from her coat pocket.*

RUTH. Oh, dear. Silly me.

DORIS gathers up RUTH's possessions. RUTH opens the compact and looks at herself in the mirror.

DORIS. I'm sorry, Miss Shaw. It's just I've been working so terribly hard and Albert don't like it and –

SYLVIA. Are you coming with me or what?

DORIS. Mrs Ellis?

As RUTH looks in the mirror, the slow hiss of static creeps in.

RUTH. 'She was killed in a revolution.'

SYLVIA. Suit yourselves.

DORIS turns to RUTH.

DORIS. Take my arm now, come on.

SYLVIA looks to GALE as she goes.

SYLVIA. What more can you say?

Exit SYLVIA.

DORIS. I'll get you home.

RUTH. Last night, David said I'd end up just like her. I thought that was terribly cruel.

DORIS. You won't, do you hear me? You won't.

RUTH. But it should have been me.

DORIS. Please, Mrs Ellis...

RUTH. Because she was... and I'm just... why, Doris... why wasn't it me?

As DORIS helps RUTH away, the static rises.

Scene Three

GALE *picks up a report from the floor.*

GALE (*reads*). 'A.C. Dalzell, Physician Superintendent, Department of Psychiatry. I interviewed Mrs Ellis for two hours on Saturday June fourth. The feature which impressed me most was her equanimity.'

As GALE *checks the open page of a dictionary,* RUTH *enters. She moves as if part of the firelight.*

RUTH. Evenness of mind or temper; composure; resignation; acceptance of fate.

RUTH *goes to the gramophone.*

GALE. 'She had drifted into a situation which was for her intolerable, she could find no way out and she has not a sufficiently hysterical personality to solve her problem by a complete loss of memory.'

RUTH *lifts the needle off the record.*

RUTH. Hysteria: Psychoneurosis with anaesthesia, convulsions, etc., usually with disturbance of moral and intellectual faculties.

GALE. 'She knew that although Blakely was, in her view, being unfaithful to her over the weekend –

RUTH *puts the needle on a new track.*

– he would return to her and she would not be able to refuse him –

'You're My Thrill' by Billie Holiday begins.

– and that this would go on and on.'

RUTH. David?

RUTH *starts to dance for* GALE, *with the detatched seduction of a stripper.*

GALE. 'She had been a successful manageress of her club... and was now living in one room because of his possessiveness and jealousy.

GALE *is hypnotised as* RUTH *removes her dress.*

Her jealousy made her hate him, although she knew she loved him.

RUTH *is beginning to falter.*

This ambivalence of emotions is a sign of... emotional immaturity.'

RUTH *collapses, her hand to her stomach.* GALE *goes to help her but* DORIS *rushes in and scoops her up in a blanket.*

DORIS. It's all right, I've got you. I'm here.

GALE *picks up his whisky and retreats to the shadows.*

Scene Four

RUTH *pulls the bloodstained blanket around her and sits among the papers.* DORIS *brings her a glass of brandy.*

RUTH. I'm sorry, I didn't know who else...

DORIS. It's no trouble, no trouble at all.

RUTH. I couldn't ask Desmond. He'd just take me back to the flat.

DORIS. And is that such a bad thing?

RUTH. I want to stay here.

DORIS. A bedsit? When you could have –

RUTH. I want to stay here.

RUTH *takes the brandy from* DORIS *and drinks with an unsteady hand.*

DORIS. When did it…?

RUTH. I don't know. Midnight? I felt… went to bed, had a horrible dream. Woke up… deep down inside… like a clenched fist that's twisting, you know? And then it's just… everywhere.

RUTH *drains her glass and hands it to* DORIS *to refill.*

Everywhere.

DORIS. I'll fetch a doctor.

RUTH. No need. It's all come away. I'll be back on my feet in a few…

RUTH *feels a wave of pain.*

DORIS. Mrs Ellis…

RUTH. I'm not going back to the nursing home.

DORIS. Who says you'll have to?

RUTH. Oh…

RUTH *reaches for* DORIS *and grips her arm.*

DORIS. I can look after you here.

RUTH. They should have cut it all out of me, taken the whole lot away.

DORIS. Breathe, now.

RUTH. They should have taken it all after Georgie…

DORIS. Breathe.

RUTH *takes a steadying breath.*

RUTH. My daughter by George. She's three now.

DORIS. I know.

RUTH. She lives with a couple he knows. Respectable people. Can't have their own children, so...

RUTH *feels the wave subside*.

DORIS. Is that better?

RUTH. I think so, don't you? Gives her more than I ever could, eh?

DORIS. I meant the pain, Mrs Ellis.

RUTH *breathes and rides out the pain*.

RUTH. And Andy's at boarding school now, don't you know?

DORIS. Yes.

RUTH. A good education. That's what a young man needs most.

DORIS. So they say.

RUTH. So I'm doing the best by them, aren't I? I'm...

RUTH *is fighting tears*.

DORIS. Now, now. He'll be home soon for Easter.

RUTH. He will, yes, I'm sure. Desmond will drive down...

DORIS. So you want to be right for the boy, Mrs Ellis.

RUTH. Ruth. Please.

RUTH *offers her glass to* DORIS.

DORIS. You want to be right.

RUTH. When's he coming, do you say? Today?

DORIS. No.

RUTH. Cos I can't have him see this. I've made such a mess of the bed.

DORIS. I'll change the sheets.

RUTH. But the mattress...

DORIS. I'll scrub it.

RUTH. The landlady, what will she say?

DORIS. Mrs... Ruth –

RUTH. I've made such a terrible mess.

RUTH *retreats into the blanket.* DORIS *refills the glass and returns it to her.*

DORIS. You don't have to stay here, you know. Not for ever. We could go away when you're back on your feet. We could go to America.

RUTH. Doris?

DORIS. New York. I've a cousin went out there. Hell's Kitchen.

RUTH. What kind of place is that?

DORIS. Ain't what it sounds. It's a whole new life, so he says.

RUTH. For two girls on their own?

DORIS. It's the land of the free.

RUTH. I couldn't leave Andy.

DORIS. The land of the three?

RUTH *manages a little laugh.*

RUTH. Yes but you've got a fella.

DORIS. He's gone.

RUTH. Gone? Where to?

DORIS. A nice girl who don't work the nights.

Beat.

RUTH. You're much better off on your own.

DORIS. I know that now. But we can't carry on as we are, can we?

RUTH. I'll be all right... I will... in the morning, I'll...

DORIS *puts her arms around* RUTH *and sings a few lines of 'God Bless the Child' to comfort her.*

When I'm modelling again...

DORIS. How you gonna do that, black and blue?

RUTH. Or perhaps I might open a shop. On a nice little high street somewhere? Maybe Essex or Kent?

DORIS. Selling...?

RUTH. Coutière.

DORIS. Clothes, ladies always want clothes.

RUTH. Can you do alterations?

DORIS. Of course.

RUTH. You could work in the back, I could...

RUTH *is distracted by a car door slamming.*

DORIS. Ruth?

RUTH. That's a car.

DORIS. What could you do, come on?

RUTH. Ssssh.

A buzzer sounds. RUTH *gets up, with difficulty.*

DORIS. Who's that at this hour?

RUTH. Help me.

DORIS. Ruth, no!

RUTH. He'll see the light on. He'll think someone's here.

DORIS. Someone is.

RUTH. He'll think it's a man.

DORIS. So?

RUTH. Help me!

The buzzer sounds again. RUTH *moves to go but* DORIS *stops her.*

DORIS. Not for him.

RUTH. I have to see him.

DORIS. You don't.

RUTH. He won't hurt me, he's come to make up.

DORIS. For what?

RUTH. We had a row, please? We fought.

DORIS. When?

RUTH. Tonight.

DORIS. With your fists?

RUTH. Doris –

DORIS. Did he hit you, Ruth?

RUTH. Answer the door.

DORIS. Answer me. Did he?

The buzzer sounds: six times in an irregular pattern.

RUTH. Yes.

DORIS. There?

DORIS puts a hand to her own stomach.

RUTH. He wanted it, Doris. But it comes down to money.

DORIS. He's got money.

RUTH. Not now. The inheritance went on the car and he can't ask his mother for someone like me.

DORIS. Ruth, you have to stop this, do you hear me?

RUTH. And I can't be poor again, Doris.

DORIS. Stop the drinking, the fighting –

RUTH. Not for him, not for anyone.

DORIS. Cos you won't have no luck till –

RUTH. I don't want luck! I want him.

The buzzer sounds: six times in an irregular pattern.

Let him in.

DORIS. What for?

RUTH. Let him in.

DORIS. Why?

RUTH. Let him in or he'll never come back. Let him in, let him
in.

RUTH *sinks to the floor.* DORIS *looks around the room; at
the mess and the blanket.*

DORIS. Perhaps it won't hurt him to see this?

RUTH. It won't. He's always so terribly sorry.

DORIS *looks back at* RUTH.

DORIS. I'll stay. I'll sleep on the floor.

RUTH. No! Just leave us alone. Let him in and please, leave us
alone.

DORIS *looks at* RUTH *and sees she means it.* DORIS
leaves. RUTH *starts to manically clear the floor of the
papers and whispers the words of 'God Bless the Child' as if
to calm herself. As she does, a camera flash blinds her. It
comes again and again from the shadows: intrusive,
exposing, disorientating.*

Static bump of a needle on a record.

RUTH *is alone in the darkness. Then comes a movement in
the black. She whispers...*

David?

GALE *is barely visible as he steps from the shadows. His
appearance is military-sharp once again. He moves slowly
and carefully towards her.*

GALE. Good Friday.

RUTH. David...

GALE. Blakely leaves. Doesn't return as he said he would.
Ruth goes to Hampstead. Watches and waits. Breaks the
windows of his car.

RUTH. David…

GALE. Saturday. Blakely doesn't return.

RUTH. David…

GALE. Sunday.

A Biblical light falls on RUTH. *A distant church bell tolls. From the static, a refrain of 'My Man'.*

GALE *slowly approaches* RUTH. *He carries an object wrapped in cloth.*

GALE *casts a lengthening shadow over* RUTH. *He crouches down next to her.*

GALE *opens the cloth to reveal a gun.*

Which man?

RUTH *looks at him and takes the gun.*

Scene Five

A prison light snaps on: harsh and bright. A bell rings: clean and clear. Keys rattle, footsteps echo and the sound of an institution fills the air. SYLVIA *and* DORIS *enter, with* DORIS *carrying a paper bag.* SYLVIA *calls over her shoulder.*

SYLVIA. Happy in your work, are you?

DORIS. Miss Shaw!

SYLVIA. It's my business what's in my handbag.

DORIS. She's only doing her job.

SYLVIA. They make you feel guilty just by –

DORIS. Look, it ain't you that's locked up here, is it?

SYLVIA. It might as well be.

Beat.

DORIS. Why? What's the matter, Miss Shaw?

Beat.

SYLVIA. Morrie's not happy. Says I should have kept her in line.

DORIS. You did. Most of the time.

SYLVIA. Did I?

DORIS. Come on, God loves a trier.

SYLVIA. God might but he don't.

RUTH *enters, in a plain civilian dress and flat shoes.*

DORIS. Ruth...

RUTH. Good morning.

DORIS. How are you, dear?

SYLVIA. How do you think?

DORIS. You look well.

RUTH. Do I?

DORIS. Yes. She looks well, don't she?

SYLVIA. Give her the bag, then.

DORIS *hands over the paper bag.*

DORIS. It's only a sewing kit. Little stuffed animals, lions and bears. Well, a sort-of a bear but what children don't know don't hurt them.

RUTH. Thank you.

DORIS. Not your children, I mean.

RUTH. No.

DORIS. Passes the time, don't it? Needlework.

RUTH. Yes. Yes it does.

Beat.

DORIS. So… you're eating and sleeping?

RUTH. They're giving me something to help.

DORIS. Do you need books or…

RUTH. I've a Bible.

DORIS. Oh, good.

RUTH. Desmond brings romantic fiction. And chocolates and flowers.

SYLVIA. In here?

DORIS. He means well, I suppose.

RUTH. Yes, he does. He does.

Beat.

DORIS. At least you can wear your own clothes.

RUTH. For now.

DORIS. And cosmetics, I see?

RUTH. The Governer's progressive.

DORIS. We wondered, Miss Shaw? We said: 'Well, it wouldn't be Ruth without all of her…', would it?

RUTH. I'd frighten the visitors, yes.

DORIS. You've had quite a few, so I'm told?

RUTH. Family and friends.

DORIS. Andy?

RUTH. He's been told I'm in Italy.

DORIS. Italy, nice.

RUTH. Modelling swimwear.

DORIS. Best not to worry the boy, eh, Miss Shaw?

SYLVIA. Has Diana been in?

RUTH. Diana?

SYLVIA. Dors.

DORIS. And you've toiletries, that sort of thing? Nightgown and underwear –

RUTH. Doris, I'm very well cared-for.

SYLVIA. Of course, dear. You've got what you want, ain'tcha?

DORIS. Miss Shaw, I told you –

SYLVIA. Front page, *Women's Mirror.* 'My Love and Hate' by Ruth Ellis.

RUTH. I don't see the papers.

SYLVIA. We don't have a choice. We 'the bores, the drunks, the have-been-and-never-will-be-celebrities'.

DORIS. Now then, I don't think we ought to –

SYLVIA. 'The lonely, jealous men at the bar.'

RUTH. I didn't say that.

SYLVIA. We'll have no business left at this rate.

RUTH. They make it all up.

SYLVIA. Do they? Your Camera Club photos are real and the *News of the World* say they'll print 'em.

RUTH. Let them. It can't hurt me now.

SYLVIA. Or your ma or your kids cos you've made it. You're famous at last.

DORIS. The girls send their love from The Little.

RUTH. That's nice.

DORIS. Lottie's had all her top teeth taken out. With the new set, they're calling her donkey.

RUTH. Poor dear.

DORIS. Have you made any friends here? Your cellmate, perhaps?

SYLVIA. It ain't Butlins.

RUTH. I'm in the hospital wing.

SYLVIA. With the lunatics?

RUTH. No.

SYLVIA. 'Only a woman could understand my state of mind.'
   Well, not this one.

DORIS. That's enough now, Miss Shaw.

SYLVIA. They're her words, not mine. 'Only a woman who led
   a similar life to mine could understand why I was irresistibly
   compelled to do what I did.'

RUTH. Like I told you –

SYLVIA. 'Irresistibly compelled.' Who do you know talks like
   that?

RUTH. No one.

SYLVIA. I'd sue 'em.

RUTH. How can I? They pay my defence.

   Beat.

SYLVIA. They what?

DORIS. Who?

RUTH. The *Daily Mirror.* They did it for Heath, Haigh and
   Christie.

DORIS. They're murderers.

SYLVIA. Doris, she shot a man six times.

DORIS. Four times. One missed, one bounced off a pavement
   and hit –

SYLVIA. Yes, we know.

RUTH. And I'm very sorry for that.

DORIS. You weren't in your right mind. You've told your legal
   man that?

RUTH. I told him the Findlaters drove us apart. How they hated me so much, they hired a nanny to lure him away.

DORIS. Ruth, that's not what –

RUTH. It is! I watched and I waited.

SYLVIA. So that's why you shot him? For some silly girl?

RUTH. But he stayed with the Findlaters –

SYLVIA. Forget the Findlaters! Who bloody gave you a gun, eh? Who gave you a gun in my club?

RUTH. Doris? Will you go to see him?

DORIS. Who?

SYLVIA. Who?

RUTH. In the chapel of rest. Take carnations.

DORIS. See...

RUTH. Red ones. Make sure they're treating him well.

SYLVIA. Oh, for Christ's sake.

DORIS. Ruth, I don't know –

SYLVIA. You're in Holloway, dear. Not Hollywood, Holloway, them bleedin' bullets were real.

RUTH. I accept what I've done.

SYLVIA. Well, I don't.

RUTH. Look, I know you're upset, with the papers –

SYLVIA. I'm upset with you! I'm upset you shot a man dead cos not one of 'em's worth what you're facing, not one.

DORIS. It's been a shock to us all, Ruth. A terrible shock.

SYLVIA. Who taught you how to look after yourself, eh? Who showed you the rules of the game?

RUTH. You did.

SYLVIA. So why didn't you come to me? Why?

RUTH. It's hard to recall.

SYLVIA. Well, you'd better start trying cos you're in one hell
of a mess.

Beat.

DORIS. Ruth? I found you a poem.

SYLVIA. A what?

DORIS *unfolds a piece of paper from her pocket.*

DORIS. I copied it down.

SYLVIA. Dear God…

DORIS. Thought it might ease your mind.

SYLVIA. She don't need a poem, she needs –

DORIS. You're not in Reading but still –

SYLVIA. Doris!

RUTH.
'For each man kills the thing he loves
Yet each man does not die.'

DORIS. You know it?

RUTH. But I'm not a man, am I?

Beat.

DORIS. And that's why they'll spare you. They won't… not a
woman… they won't, Miss Shaw, will they?

SYLVIA *gets up to leave.*

SYLVIA. I've got a club to run. For the time being, at least.

DORIS. Just stay a minute.

SYLVIA. I don't care for being closed in.

RUTH. Of course. Thank you for coming. Sylvie?

Beat.

SYLVIA. I thought I'd seen it all. Suppose I have now.

RUTH. The papers… I had no idea… I didn't think.

SYLVIA. You girls never do.

RUTH. Well, sometimes that's for the best; but forgive me.

Beat.

SYLVIA. It's done now, ain't it?

RUTH. And thank you for all you… for Vickie and I.

SYLVIA. I did nothing.

RUTH. She's with us, you know? She's here now.

SYLVIA. Don't turn in on yourself, do you hear me?

RUTH. I won't.

SYLVIA. Keep…

RUTH. What?

DORIS. Miss Shaw?

Beat.

SYLVIA. Morrie be damned.

RUTH. Beg your pardon?

SYLVIA. When you get out, you've a job and a room.
However… whenever… all right?

RUTH. Yes.

SYLVIA. I'll see you.

SYLVIA *cups* RUTH*'s face in her hand.*

I'll see you.

Exit SYLVIA, *watched by* RUTH.

RUTH. She was right about David. You all were. But so was I.

DORIS. What do you mean?

RUTH. He carried a flagon of ale from the pub. It ran down the
hill where he bled. Quite a sight to be left with… a foaming
great river of red.

DORIS. You're not to blame for this, Ruth.

RUTH. Then who is?

DORIS. A man in the newspaper says it's society.

RUTH. I've never been part of society. I've always relied on myself.

DORIS. *The Times* and the *Telegraph* write of you, too. I'm keeping the cuttings –

RUTH. That's nice.

DORIS. I'll do all that's necessary. Go to the chapel, the police, I'll get you whatever you need.

RUTH. Yes. Peroxide.

DORIS. Peroxide?

RUTH. I can't go to court with my roots.

DORIS. But shouldn't you perhaps…

RUTH. What?

DORIS. Look more like you're sorry?

RUTH. I'm not.

DORIS. Ruth…

RUTH. It's the Old Bailey, dear. Wouldn't you?

Scene Six

A barrage of press cameras flash at RUTH *and she hears Billie Holiday's 'T'ain't Nobody's Business' in a fractured, repeating phrase, as if on a scratched record.*

The cacophony ends with the sound of a judge's gavel, knocking six times in an irregular pattern.

GALE *emerges from the shadows. The summer heat is rising.*

GALE. From the bowels of the building, she came. Black two-piece suit, astrakhan collar. White blouse, platinum hair. Spike heels on the court-room floor, stage whisper up in the gallery: 'Blonde tart.'

VICKIE *emerges with a prison uniform. She helps* RUTH *to dress and playfully gives voice to the court.*

RUTH *is in a kind of daydream, with* VICKIE *a comforting distraction from the difficult questions.*

VICKIE *(as Judge).* Ruth Ellis, you are charged that on the tenth of April last you murdered David Moffett Drummond Blakely. How say you, are you guilty or not guilty?

GALE. Her plea follows legal advice.

RUTH. Not guilty.

GALE. The jury: two women, ten men.

VICKIE. Members of the jury, you will approach this case without any thought of sympathy either for the man –

RUTH. He was a very likeable person, Your Honour.

VICKIE. Or the accused, who is a young woman, you might think, treated badly by the deceased.

RUTH. I got very attached to him.

VICKIE. You will arrive at the verdict fearlessly.

RUTH. He only hit me with his hands and fists but I bruise very easily.

VICKIE. Without any thought of the consequence one way or another.

RUTH. We had a fight a few days previously. I don't know whether that caused the miscarriage but he did thump me in the tummy.

GALE (*steps forward*). Ellis?

RUTH. Inspector?

GALE. What man? Which club?

RUTH. I don't recall.

GALE. What did he look like?

Beat.

RUTH. Ordinary.

GALE. Ordinary?

RUTH. Average, you know?

VICKIE. Chignon.

RUTH. Hollywood.

GALE. Ellis!

RUTH. I've nothing to say.

VICKIE *vies with* GALE *for* RUTH's *attention.*

VICKIE. In this case, six shots were fired by a Smith and Wesson revolver.

GALE. You give him a loan –

VICKIE. A lethal weapon.

GALE. He leaves you a gun.

VICKIE. Three or four shots were fired into the body.

GALE. For what purpose?

VICKIE. One was fired at extremely close range.

RUTH *watches as* VICKIE *points an imaginary gun to a body on the floor.*

GALE. Ellis!

RUTH *snaps out of the vision.*

RUTH. Security. For the loan.

GALE. What's wrong with a wristwatch?

RUTH. He gave it to me so I took it, that's all.

GALE. Doris Judd's been to see me. She's given a statement. She says on the record, if you'd had a gun she'd have known.

RUTH. How?

VICKIE. If you are satisfied –

GALE. She helped you to pack when you left. From The Court, The Little –

RUTH. She's not privy to all of my secrets.

GALE. There's more?

VICKIE. If you are satisfied that Mrs Ellis *intentionally* fired the shots –

GALE. Cussen.

VICKIE. Then that would amount to a verdict of guilty of murder –

GALE. Desmond Cussen.

VICKIE. If you are left in *reasonable doubt* whether, at the time she fired those shots, she intended to kill or do grievous bodily harm –

GALE. When did he last come to see you?

VICKIE. You will find her guilty –

GALE. Has he been in since the trial –

VICKIE. Of manslaughter.

RUTH *turns away from* VICKIE.

RUTH. He's found it all rather difficult.

GALE. I'll say. He was white as a sheet in the witness box.

RUTH. Wouldn't you be?

GALE. Not if my conscience was clear.

RUTH. Desmond's a gentleman.

GALE. What does that mean?

RUTH. Well, if you don't know by now –

VICKIE (*as QC*). Mrs Ellis!

RUTH. Yes?

VICKIE. When you went to Hampstead with that gun in your bag, what was your intention?

RUTH. It was obvious…

GALE. Ellis, listen to me.

RUTH. It was obvious that when I shot him, I intended to kill him.

VICKIE. No further questions.

GALE. Cussen gave you that gun on the Easter weekend.

RUTH. No further questions.

GALE. He gave you the gun and drove you to Hampstead.

RUTH. That's not true, I rode in a taxi.

GALE. So why hasn't the driver come forward? Nice-looking blonde in the back?

RUTH. Not all men are like you.

GALE. Not all fares are famous.

RUTH. I wasn't that night. I was no one.

   Beat.

VICKIE. 'Talk about the glamorous life of a mannequin.'

Beat.

GALE. The revolver was stripped down and oiled. Who did that for you, Mrs Ellis?

RUTH. I'm guilty. I'm rather…

GALE. Who?

VICKIE (*as Judge*). Members of the jury; if you are satisfied that at the time she fired those shots, she had the intention of killing or doing grievous bodily harm, then your *duty* is to find her guilty of wilful murder.

RUTH. I was just…

GALE. Just…?

RUTH *looks from* GALE *to* VICKIE.

RUTH. I was just very upset.

VICKIE. I know, dear. I know.

VICKIE *fades into the shadows. When* RUTH *turns to* GALE, *we are now in real time: July 12th, 1955.*

RUTH *is dressed in her prison uniform.*

GALE. Mrs Ellis, we've got our conviction. I shouldn't even be here.

RUTH. Then go home to your wife.

GALE. I don't have a wife.

RUTH. Well, go out and get laid, I know girls.

GALE. I know girls. And I know when they're lying.

RUTH. Inspector, I'm terribly tired.

GALE. Easter Sunday.

RUTH. Please, if you don't mind –

GALE. You went out with Desmond and Andy.

RUTH. No more.

GALE. Where to?

Beat.

RUTH. London Zoo.

GALE. And you came home –

RUTH. Depressed. Sad flamingos, can't stand 'em.

GALE. You came home with Cussen.

RUTH. And asked him to go. Put Andy to bed. I hadn't slept, two nights straight and… what time will they come for me, sir? Tomorrow.

GALE. I can't discuss that.

RUTH. But no one else will.

RUTH *holds his gaze.*

GALE. Nine o'clock sharp.

RUTH. Who'll be present?

GALE. The Governor, the doctor, the nurse. Two warders.

RUTH. My particular warders?

GALE. The prison chaplain.

RUTH. And it's Mr Pierrepont, I presume? I read about him in the *News of the World*, when what's-his-name… Bentley… was done.

GALE. It is.

RUTH. How far will he take me, Inspector? Is it a very long walk?

GALE *looks across the cell and back to* RUTH.

GALE. The wardrobe? They'll move it. Behind, there's a door which they'll open and…

RUTH. Oh.

RUTH *looks across the cell*.

GALE. You're twenty-eight years old, Mrs Ellis –

RUTH. How long will it take?

Beat.

GALE. Nine seconds, they tell me, that's all.

RUTH *takes* GALE *by the wrist and looks at his watch*.

RUTH. One, two, three… (*And counts mentally to nine*.) No worse than having a tooth out.

RUTH *lets go of* GALE'*s wrist*.

GALE. You're a mother.

RUTH. They'll bury me here, I suppose? No headstone, that's fine. Morbid things, if you ask me, aren't they?

GALE. Your son is ten years old.

RUTH. Yes, and he's very well cared-for. He boards at an excellent school.

GALE. Who pays the fees?

RUTH. That's my business.

GALE. Is it? You've brokered a deal?

RUTH. No.

GALE. 'Look after the boy and I'll look after you.'

RUTH. You make me sound very mysterious.

GALE. I think it's perfectly clear.

RUTH. And I've told you, it's not your concern.

Beat.

GALE. I spoke to him.

RUTH. Desmond?

GALE. Andy.

RUTH. You had no right.

GALE. He says he did spend the day at the zoo. On his own.

RUTH. When did you speak to him? How?

GALE. And that night, he remembers you went out in black. So
  does your housekeeper, black two-piece suit. When we
  brought you in, you wore grey.

  Beat.

RUTH. He's wrong.

GALE. We raise our children to tell us the truth.

RUTH. The truth…

GALE. It could bring a reprieve, even now.

RUTH. The truth is, I'd get life. Twenty-five years to wither and
  rot, to go dried-up and bitter and sour. To lie in a single bed
  thinking of –

GALE. Freedom, eventually.

RUTH. Freedom, yes. Four in the morning. Out of our minds.
  The way they say opium feels, or Heaven. We had it, see?
  David and I. For a few moments, at least.

  The rising sound of a chanting crowd.

CROWD. *Ellis – Ellis – Ellis!*

GALE. There's hundreds out there. Thousands more in the
  cities and towns –

RUTH. I don't want a white knight to save me, Inspector.

GALE. I swear that's the last thing I am.

  RUTH *looks at* GALE *and smiles.*

RUTH. Still…

GALE. What?

RUTH. You've done all right for yourself. Getting so high in
  the ranks.

GALE. I'm like you. I worked hard, that's all.

CROWD. *Ellis – Ellis – Ellis!*

RUTH. South London boy?

GALE. Brixton.

RUTH. Done well to get out of there, too.

GALE. Thank the Army for that.

RUTH. Active service?

GALE. Oh, yes.

RUTH. I had a wonderful war. Danced every night.

GALE. Well, that's what we fought for.

RUTH. I met a GI from Quebec. Clare Andrea McCallum. He bought me carnations. Gave me a son. Said: 'We'll marry for sure, ma'am.' Turned out he already was.

GALE. Not a war hero, then?

RUTH. No, sir.

GALE. I'm sorry.

RUTH. Don't be. Can't waltz through life for ever, can you?

   RUTH *gestures to an imaginary dance floor.*

GALE. What?

RUTH. While I'm still flesh and blood.

   From the static comes 'Guilty' by Billie Holiday.

GALE. Ruth…

RUTH. Jack.

   RUTH *and* GALE *dance together.*

   RUTH *looks at* GALE.

   For the record, Inspector. That's all.

   GALE *takes out his pocketbook.*

GALE. Ruth Ellis, you have been advised to tell the whole truth in regard to the circumstances leading up to the killing of David Blakely...

GALE *nods to* RUTH.

RUTH. And it's only with the greatest reluctance I've decided to tell how it was that I... that I got the gun with which I shot him.

GALE. In your own words.

GALE *makes notes*.

RUTH. I didn't do so before because I felt that I was needlessly getting someone into possible trouble.

GALE. Go on.

RUTH. I'd been drinking Pernod. P – E – R – N...

GALE. O – D.

RUTH. I think that's how it's spelt... in Desmond Cussen's flat. He'd been drinking too. This was about eight-thirty p.m. We'd been drinking for some time. I'd been telling Desmond about Blakely's treatment of me. I was in a terribly depressed state.

GALE. And then?

RUTH. All I remember is Desmond gave me a loaded gun. He was jealous of David, as in fact David was of him. I'd say they hated each other but I... but I was in such a dazed state, I can't remember what was said. I rushed out as soon as he gave me the gun, he stayed in the flat. I rushed back after a second or two and said: 'Will you drive me to Hampstead?' He did so and left me at the top of Tanza Road.

GALE. And the gun? Had you seen it before?

RUTH. The only gun I'd ever seen there was a small air pistol used as a game with a target.

GALE. Is there anything more you wish to say?

RUTH. No, sir. That's all.

GALE *goes back over his notes as* RUTH *kneels to pray.*
The Prayer of the Penitent weaves in and around GALE.

The crowd chant throughout.

CROWD. *Justice for Ellis! Justice for Ellis!*

RUTH. Oh my God, I am heartily sorry for having offended
Thee.

GALE. Method, analysis, logic.

RUTH. And I detest all my sins because I dread the loss of
Heaven and the pains of Hell.

GALE. Method, analysis, logic.

RUTH. But most of all because they offend Thee, my God, who
are all good and deserving of all my love.

GALE *looks to the audience.*

GALE. The statement was typed up and signed.

RUTH. I firmly resolve –

GALE. It went straight to the Home Office.

RUTH. With the help of Thy grace –

GALE. We went to find Cussen.

RUTH. To confess my sins –

GALE. He'd had a tip-off and fled.

RUTH. To do penance –

GALE. There was a national petition.

RUTH. And to amend my life, thanks to the Lord, for He is
good –

GALE. Newspapers calling for mercy.

RUTH. His mercy endures for ever.

GALE. It wasn't enough.

The sound of a chanting crowd rises.

CROWD. *Justice for Ellis! Justice for Ellis! Ellis, Ellis, Ellis, Ellis, Ellis, Ellis, Ellis!*

A church bell strikes nine.

RUTH *rises, takes off her spectacles and turns to* GALE.

RUTH. I won't be needing these any more.

GALE *takes the spectacles and steps back.*

The crowd fall silent.

RUTH *stands.*

Raises her chin.

Closes her eyes.

The sound of a lever.

A trapdoor.

The ninth chime strikes.

RUTH *is gone.*

Scene Seven

'I'll Be Seeing You' by Billie Holiday.

DORIS *folds white napkins.*

SYLVIA *counts a handful of pound notes.*

DORIS *looks across to* SYLVIA *and catches her eye.*

DORIS *gives a half-smile, which* SYLVIA *returns.*

SYLVIA *crosses the floor and meets* GALE.

GALE *nods.* SYLVIA *returns the nod.*

GALE *takes* RUTH's *spectacles from his pocket and offers them to* SYLVIA.

SYLVIA *takes the spectacles.*

SYLVIA *leaves with a touch to his arm.*

DORIS *follows her with her napkins, glancing at* GALE.

GALE *glances heavenward and continues on his way.*

The songs plays out until all that is left is static.

The End.

A Nick Hern Book

The Thrill of Love first published in Great Britain as a paperback original in 2013 by Nick Hern Books Limited, The Glasshouse, 49a Goldhawk Road, London W12 8QP, in association with the New Vic Theatre

Cover image: © Corbis
Image design: Candida Kelsall
Cover design: Ned Hoste, 2H

Typeset by Nick Hern Books, London
Printed in Great Britain by CPI Group (UK) Ltd

A CIP catalogue record for this book is available from the British Library

ISBN 978 1 84842 316 9